The United States and Iran

William Spencer

Twenty-First Century Books
Brookfield, Connecticut

Published by Twenty-First Century Books
A Division of The Millbrook Press, Inc.
2 Old New Milford Road
Brookfield, Connecticut 06804
www.millbrookpress.com

Photographs courtesy of The Granger Collection, New York: p. 18; Archive
Photos: pp. 22, 97, 107 (© Reuters/Faith Saribas), 111 (© Reuters/Aladin Abdel
Naby); Corbis/Hulton-Deutsch Collection: p. 25; Presbyterian Historical Society,
Presbyterian Church (U.S.A.) (Philadelphia): p. 30; Culver Pictures, Inc.: p. 33;
Corbis/Bettmann-UPI: pp. 40, 80, 90; AP/Wide World Photos: pp. 59, 61, 82, 88;
© Hulton Getty/Liaison Agency: pp. 69, 103; Corbis: p. 73; National Archives:
p. 78; Liaison Agency: p. 101 (© Francois Lochon). Maps by Jeff Ward.

Library of Congress Cataloging-in-Publication Data
Spencer, William, 1922-
The United States and Iran/William Spencer.
p. cm.
Includes bibliographical references (p.   ) and index.
Summary: Examines the history of relations between the United States and Iran
and the various shifts in Iranian government that have affected those relations.
ISBN 0-7613-1554-3 (lib. bdg.)
1. United States—Relations—Iran Juvenile literature. 2. Iran—Relations—United
States Juvenile literature. 3. Iran—Politics and government 4. Juvenile literature.
[1. United States—Relations—Iran. 2. Iran—Relations—United States. 3. Iran—
Politics and government.] I. Title.
E183.8.I55S64   2000   327.73055—dc21   99-41426 CIP

Contents

Introduction Persia or Iran?

I n 1979 a band of youths in a far-off country scaled the walls of the American Embassy in its capital city, occupied the Embassy, and took fifty-three American staff members prisoner, holding them as hostages for 444 days. This event brought that far-off country and its people into full view of the American public. Citizens were glued to their TV sets for daily reports, and many households hung yellow ribbons on their front doors to show their support for the imprisoned Americans. In that country, in contrast, there were seemingly endless parades of demonstrators carrying banners in an unknown language and shouting, "Down with America, the Great Satan!"

Who were (and are) these people who dared to defy the mighty United States and hold its citizens as hostages? Today we know them as Iranians and their land as Iran. But not very long ago the Western world knew them as Persians, and their country as Persia. Which is correct, and is the difference important?

One way to settle this question is by learning what the people of Persia/Iran call themselves and their land. In their language it is called Iran-zamin, "the land of Iran." This land has been settled for five to six thousand years. In ancient times other peoples living in the area of the present-day Middle East used "Iran" as a geographical and linguistic term, but used the term "Persian" to describe certain tribes that had migrated into a particular part of this region, known to them as "Pars" (or "Parsua" in some languages). The tribes were referred to as "people of Pars"—in its modern form, Persians.

In the Old Testament of the Bible and the historical writings of Judaism there are many references to the Persians and the empire they established twenty-five centuries ago. But after their empire broke up and other peoples came to dominate the Middle East, the Western world pretty much lost contact with the Persians and their land. For almost five centuries the Western world was controlled by the Roman Empire, and after this empire broke up, the nations of Western Europe gradually developed into their present form.

In the nineteenth century these European nations entered a period of great economic and technological expansion, a period called the Industrial Revolution. European military leaders developed new and more powerful weapons for their armies, weapons that paved the way for the missiles and nuclear arms of today. Their rulers, notably those of Great Britain, France, and later Russia and Germany, began moving into other parts of the world in search of sources of raw materials for their industries and factories and for energy to run their ships, trains, and eventually their cars and airplanes. Because of their new weapons European armies were superior to the armies of Asian and African rulers and easily defeated them. By the end of the nineteenth century most of Africa, the Middle East, India, and other Asian lands were under direct or indirect European control.

The process by which Iran came under European control and then gradually recovered its independence and national pride with the help of the United States will be dealt with in later chapters of this book. But it is important to note that by the mid-nineteenth century the names "Persia" and "Persians" had become negative terms. Europeans who came in contact with them generally considered them an ignorant and socially inferior people living in a backward, primitive country.

In the 1930s, Reza Shah, the Iranian ruler, wished to restore his people's national pride and dignity and prove to the world that his country was no longer backward and inferior compared with the nations of Europe. Accordingly, he issued an edict making Iran the country's official name. Then in 1971 his son and successor, Mohammed Reza Shah, invited world leaders to a celebration marking the 2,500th anniversary of the monarchy in Iran. He informed them that the country's legal name was Iran. Although "Persia" and "Persians" are sometimes used by people in Western countries (notably in Great Britain), for the people of Iran they are terms that recall the ancient past when their ancestors ruled a mighty empire. The one exception is the use of "Persian" for the Persian Gulf, the large and strategically important body of water extending southward from the Iranian and Arabian seacoasts to the territory of the United Arab Emirates (see map). This usage is geographical rather than political, derived from the nineteenth-century conflicts of European states over territory and resources in the Middle East.

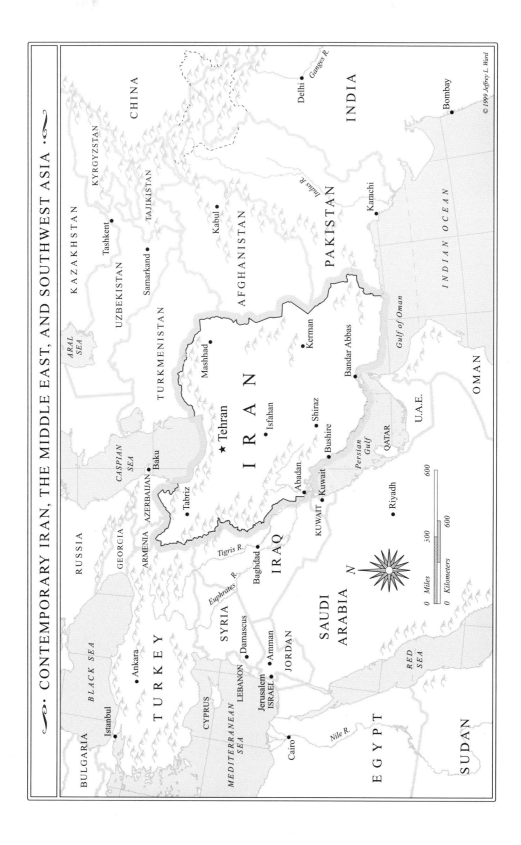

∾ • CONTEMPORARY IRAN, THE MIDDLE EAST, AND SOUTHWEST ASIA • ∾

© 1999 Jeffrey L. Ward

CHINA

KAZAKHSTAN

KYRGYZSTAN

Tashkent

UZBEKISTAN

TAJIKISTAN

Samarkand

TURKMENISTAN

ARAL SEA

Mashhad

Kabul

AFGHANISTAN

Delhi

Ganges R.

INDIA

Bombay

PAKISTAN

Karachi

Indus R.

Kerman

Bandar Abbas

Gulf of Oman

INDIAN OCEAN

OMAN

CASPIAN SEA

Baku

AZERBAIJAN

Tabriz

I R A N

★ Tehran

Isfahan

Shiraz

Bushire

U.A.E.

QATAR

Persian Gulf

RUSSIA

GEORGIA

ARMENIA

Abadan

Kuwait

KUWAIT

Riyadh

Tigris R.

Baghdad

IRAQ

Euphrates R.

SYRIA

SAUDI ARABIA

N

TURKEY

Ankara

BLACK SEA

Damascus

Amman

JORDAN

BULGARIA

Istanbul

CYPRUS

LEBANON

Jerusalem

ISRAEL

MEDITERRANEAN SEA

RED SEA

EGYPT

Cairo

Nile R.

SUDAN

0 Miles 300 600

0 Kilometers 600

Chapter 1 Superpower into Nation

The first official contact between the United States and Iran was in 1856, when representatives of the two governments signed a Treaty of Friendship and Commerce. But by then Iran was already a very old nation, with a history spanning more than 2,500 years. The United States, in contrast, had been an independent nation for barely seventy-five years! The difference between the two nations in the way they then viewed each other (and themselves) shows clearly in the language of the Preamble of the Treaty:

> The President of the United States and His Majesty as exalted as the Planet Saturn; Whose splendor and magnificence are equal to that of the Skies; The Monarch whose armies are as numerous as the Stars; The Sublime Emperor of all Persia; being desirous of establishing relations of friendship between their two governments, have agreed on the following. . . . [1]

At that time the United States was almost unknown to most of the world's peoples as an independent nation. Iran, in contrast, was at various times in its long history a powerful nation, ruled by Shahs (kings, in the Persian language). At times these rulers controlled most of the lands of the present-day Middle East. When its rulers were weak and ineffective, Iran's strategic location astride the major trade routes from Europe across Asia to India and China made it a target for invasions from outside. But even powerful foreign invaders were eventually absorbed by the Iranians. As a result, Iran has been able to preserve its own language, culture, and national identity throughout its long history.

The development of the Persian language, commonly called Farsi from association with the original homeland of the Persian tribes ("Fars" or "Pars"), illustrates the skill of the Iranians at absorbing these foreign influences. Thus the Arab conquest brought Arabic letters and sounds, which were added to the original Farsi to preserve it as a distinct language, while expansion into neighboring areas resulted in a number of Farsi-related dialects and languages such as Pushtu, the major language of Afghanistan.

In this respect, Iran and the United States share a similar experience. Each has been a "melting pot" into which foreign influences and ideas, as well as foreign peoples, have been absorbed to form a nation with a distinct identity. But in another way the nations are very different. The majority of those who settled the land that became the United States were fleeing from religious or political persecution or economic misfortune. For them America was a shining New World, with economic opportunity and freedom of religion. Since the United States was formed as an independent nation, it has been led by presidents elected by the people and governed under principles set out in its Constitution. The Constitution provides for a national legislature (Congress) elected by the people to make the laws, a Bill of Rights that guarantees basic human rights for all citizens, and a legal system with various levels of courts to ensure that these laws reflect the common good.

Iran's political system developed in a different way from that of the United States. In Iran, religion and politics have always been interlinked. Until the 1979 revolution that ended the monarchy, Iran's rulers based their authority ultimately on the principle of the divine right to rule. This principle holds that God, or some all-powerful being, has entrusted authority and power over His people to certain rulers to whom He has given the right to rule. Iran's rulers, whether they were emperors, sultans, or Shahs, believed that they possessed this right. The democratic process did not exist for them. With the 1979 revolution and establishment of the Islamic Republic, the "divine right of kings" was replaced by the "divine right" of the religious leaders to rule. Monarchy became theocracy, and the right to rule was entrusted to a supreme religious leader as the final authority under God.

One other important factor in Iran's relations with other nations stems from the fact that when its rulers were weak it was often invaded. The weakness of nineteenth-century rulers faced with European power led them to seek the friendship and support of the United States. They hoped by allying themselves with a new and strong nation, one too far away to be a threat to them, they would be able to ward off the threat of European occupations.

The First Superpower

The Iranians first appear in history as a group of nomadic tribes. Their original homeland was in central Asia, but some three thousand years ago they migrated into the Iranian Plateau and settled there. There were two main tribal groups, the Medes and the Persians. The Medes settled in various areas, while the Persians were concentrated in Pars, in what is now central southwestern Iran. Both Medes and Persians took part in the wars and rivalries of such ancient Middle Eastern peoples as the Sumerians, Akkadians, Assyrians, and Babylonians. In the sixth century B.C.E., a Persian tribal chief, Cyrus, united the Medes and Persians and overcame most of the peoples of the area, founding the world's first true empire, a vast territory inhabited by many different peoples who were ruled by a single all-powerful ruler.

Cyrus and his successors headed the first world "superpower." Their empire extended from Egypt and Anatolia (modern Turkey) across the Middle East and southern Asia to the borders of India and China (see map). It was also a superpower in it organization and management. It had the first postal service, with couriers on fast horses who could deliver mail in relays to any point in the empire within a week. A network of spies kept watch in towns and cities to report unrest or possible invasions to the emperor and his officials. As the empire expanded, conquered territories were divided into provinces called *satrapies*, each with an appointed governor who collected taxes, administered justice, and organized troop contingents for the imperial armies in time of war. This ancient

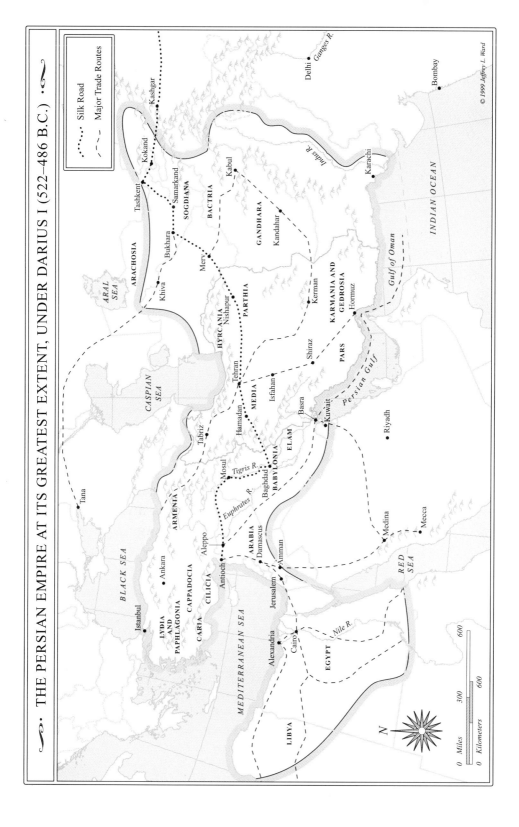

THE PERSIAN EMPIRE AT ITS GREATEST EXTENT, UNDER DARIUS I (522–486 B.C.)

Silk Road
Major Trade Routes

© 1999 Jeffrey L. Ward

BLACK SEA

CASPIAN SEA

ARAL SEA

MEDITERRANEAN SEA

RED SEA

Persian Gulf

Gulf of Oman

INDIAN OCEAN

Nile R.

Tigris R.

Euphrates R.

Indus R.

Ganges R.

Istanbul
Ankara
Tana
Tabriz
Tashkent
Kokand
Kashgar
Samarkand
Bukhara
Khiva
Merv
Nishapur
Tehran
Hamadan
Mosul
Baghdad
Isfahan
Shiraz
Kerman
Kabul
Kandahar
Hormuz
Basra
Kuwait
Riyadh
Medina
Mecca
Amman
Damascus
Jerusalem
Aleppo
Antioch
Cairo
Alexandria
Karachi
Bombay
Delhi

LYDIA AND PAPHLAGONIA
CAPPADOCIA
CARIA
CILICIA
ARMENIA
ARABIA
EGYPT
LIBYA
BABYLONIA
ELAM
MEDIA
HYRCANIA
PARTHIA
PARS
KARMANIA AND GEDROSIA
ARACHOSIA
SOGDIANA
BACTRIA
GANDHARA

N

0   300   600 Miles
0   600   Kilometers

imperial system has always been a source of great pride for Iranians. The fact that they can look back on a time when their nation ruled most of the known world gives them an inner belief in their superiority over other peoples.

The Birth of a Nation

The Persian Empire was overthrown in 333 B.C.E. by the army of Alexander the Great, a king of Macedonia in northern Greece who set out to conquer the world. He probably would have done so, but he died unexpectedly at the age of thirty-three, and his lands were divided up among his generals. For a century there was a power vacuum in the former empire as tribal chiefs and Alexander's generals vied for power. Eventually the Parthians, a tribe from Pars, established a separate kingdom in Iran.

After the Roman Empire was established in the Middle East, Parthia became its greatest rival. Roman legionnaires were often unable to catch up with the swift-riding Parthian horse-archers, who could shoot arrows with deadly effect riding backward. In one famous battle the Parthians destroyed an entire Roman army of 40,000 men.

Later Parthian rulers were often weak and ineffective, and four centuries after they had seized power in Persia they were overthrown by the Sassanians, a new and vigorous tribe from another province. The Sassanians continued the rivalry with Rome with equal success, expanding their territory until it was nearly as vast as the empire of Cyrus and his successors. And their control of land and sea-trade routes across the

Middle East to India and China (the famous "Silk Road") brought much wealth into Iran.

The greatest Sassanian ruler was Khosrow I (A.D. 531–579). He was known as "The Just," and is a model for Iranians even today as a wise, just, and tolerant leader. One of his edicts reads: "A just king is ordained by Ahura Mazda [the god of truth and light, in the Zoroastrian religion]. He rules so that the empire will prosper, the common people will be freed from fear and will enjoy a good life, science will advance, culture will be looked after, men will be generous, just, and gracious."[2]

Religion in Iran

Throughout their history Iranians have sought after, accepted, and rejected many different religions. It may be that like the Indians of the American Southwest, Iranians have been inspired by their vast, rugged, and starkly beautiful landscape to reflect upon the divine power that they believe created the universe and then mankind. Whatever the reason, the influence of religion on daily life in Iran is clearly visible. In the personal greetings and conversations of people (which include frequent references to God), and in daily prayers, visits to saints' tombs, and requests for intercession in cases of illness or other human problems, Iranians reveal how important religion is in their lives.

This concern with religion is not new. From the time of the Persian Empire, rulers called on Ahura Mazda for guidance to help them rule justly. Conversely, unjust rulers were said to be controlled by Ahriman, the spirit of evil, giving their subjects the right to overthrow them. Under the Sassanians, Zoroastrianism, a dualistic religion developed by the prophet Zoroaster and centered on the contest between good and evil for men's souls, became the official religion of Iran. Certain priests were made responsible for tending the sacred fire that was always kept burning in Zoroastrian temples. Fire was the symbol of Ahura Mazda, and Zoroastrians believed that if the sacred fire went out, the world would end with the triumph of evil over good. But as long as it burned there would be justice for the people under their rulers.

The Rise of Islam

Zoroaster's teachings and those of a later Christian prophet, Mani, had much influence over the religious orientation of the Iranians. Theirs is a deeply religious worldview. One writer has said of them that "they are as prolific in creating and refining religions as they are in creating beautiful objects of cloth, metal, wood, and stone," meaning that their artistic craftsmanship is also deeply spiritual.[3] Zoroaster's concern with the individual's obligation to work for good against evil, and Mani's desire to bring all peoples together in peace and harmony under God (the essence of Manichaeism), form the bedrock of the religious understanding and worldview of the Iranians.

The most important religious influence on Iran's people came to them from the outside world. It was brought not by wandering scholars or missionaries but by a conquering army. This army came from Arabia, a vast, largely desert region geographically close to Iran but inhabited by a nomadic people whom the sophisticated, civilized Iranians considered mere savages.

These Arab conquerors brought with them a new religion, one different from Zoroastrianism or Manichaeism (although it shared many things with Judaism and Christianity, religions well known to the Iranians, few of them accepted these faiths). The name of this new religion was Islam, meaning "surrender" or "submission" to God in Arabic, the language of Arabia. Those who submit to the will of God are known as *Muslims*. There are about 900 million Muslims in the world today, 3 million in the United States and 64 million in Iran. But prior to the 7th century A.D., there were none anywhere in the world.

Islam was founded by a merchant and trader named Muhammad, who lived in the small city of Mecca, in southwestern Arabia. He lived from A.D. 570 to 632. Muhammad was highly respected for his honesty, his business skills, and especially for his ability to mediate conflicts and settle disputes. Like his near contemporary the Sassanian monarch Khosrow I, he was known as al-Amin ("the Just"). Muslims believe that because of these qualities he was chosen by God to be a messenger to bring God's word to the Arabs and ultimately to the entire world.

In his fortieth year Muhammad received the first in a series of messages from God, via the angel Gabriel, while meditating, as was his custom, in a cave near Mecca. These messages "revealed" God's plan for the redemption of mankind. That is why they are usually called "revelations." After Muhammad's death they were collected and written down in book form as the Koran (Al-Qur'an, in Arabic), the Holy Book of Islam. Muslims believe that the Koran is the literal word of God and follow its teachings as their guide not only in their spiritual lives but also in daily behavior.

This Arabic print shows the prophet Muhammed

with Ali, his son-in-law, and Ali's sons.

During Muhammad's ministry the only Muslims in the world were his few followers in Arabia. But Islam was, and is, intended for all peoples every-

---

**The Five Pillars (so-called because
they support the "House of Islam"):**

1. **The Confession of Faith—I swear there is no God
   but God, and Muhammad is the Messenger of God**

2. **Prayer, five times daily at prescribed intervals**

3. **Fasting for a full month, the month of the first reve-
   lation (Ramadan)**

4. **Almsgiving or tithing to support the House of God**

5. **Pilgrimage at least once in one's lifetime to Mecca,
   Islam's holy city**

---

where. On the surface it is a simple faith, with few
basic requirements.

After Muhammad's death the Muslim Arabs were
inspired to go out and convert all peoples to what they
believed was the true faith. Their armies swept out of
Arabia with lightning speed, and within a few years
the hand of Islam reached from Morocco in a broad
band across northern Africa, the Middle East, Iran,
Afghanistan, and central Asia to the borders of India
and China.

Iran's turn came early. In 637 an Arab army over-
ran the Sassanian forces in the Battle of Qadisiya (kah-
DEE-shee-yah), another of history's turning points.
The Sassanian ruler was killed, and Iran became part
of a vast Islamic empire. The spiritual and temporal
head of this empire was the caliph, a title in Arabic
meaning variously "agent," "deputy," or "representative." Inasmuch as Muhammad had been the messenger and agent of God during his lifetime, the caliphs

who carried on his ministry served as agents of Muhammad, ruling over many peoples whose only unifying bond was Islam.

Sunnis and Shia

But the spiritual unity of Islam was not matched by political unity. Disagreement arose early within the Muslim community over the question of leadership. Muhammad had fallen ill and died suddenly, probably from pneumonia, in 632. He left no will, no instructions as to a successor, and as he had been their only leader, the distraught Muslims did not know what to do. After much discussion they turned to tribal custom and elected Muhammad's father-in-law, the senior member of the community, as the first caliph.

The election was by majority vote, but a vocal minority argued that only members of Muhammad's immediate family were qualified to lead the community because they shared his insight and understanding of God's purpose. This minority called itself *Shia*, an Arabic word meaning "Party of ." They argued that Ali, Muhammad's cousin, his son-in-law, and father of his two surviving grandsons, should have been chosen caliph, and his sons after him. For this reason the Shia are always called the Party of Ali (*Shi'at Ali*). Ever since that time 1,400 years ago, the Shia have remained in opposition to the majority of Muslims. They believe that Ali, his sons, and thereafter their male descendants are the rightful leaders of the community of Muslims, but that they have been deprived of that right by the majority, for political reasons. It is a dispute that would have important consequences for Iran in later years.

High Tide of Islam

For six hundred years after the Arab conquest, Iran was part of a unified Islamic empire headed by the caliphs. Having already developed a high level of civilization, Iranians made many important contributions to the building of a truly great Islamic civilization, one that was the envy of the rest of the world. Scholars from Iran and other Islamic lands made important discoveries and advances in medicine, chemistry, physics, astronomy, and other scientific fields. Muslims translated the great works of Greek and other classical philosophers, geographers, and others into Arabic; thus preserving them for transmittal to European societies through the great libraries of medieval Islamic Spain. In the arid Middle East, Muslim engineers developed irrigation systems to compensate for the lack of rainfall and to enable farmers to reap dependable harvests from their food crops. Many important foods that we depend on today, such as oranges, lemons, coffee, and tea, were brought to our ancestors by Islamic agricultural experts. At a time when London and Paris were villages of mud huts and muddier streets and New York City did not exist, Baghdad and other Islamic cities were models of urban comfort and design, with fine parks, hospitals, sports arenas, schools, and libraries.

The Mongol Conquest

In the thirteenth century, this splendid civilization came crashing down in ruins, destroyed by an army of small wiry men on tireless shaggy horses from central Asia. They were the Mongols, non-Muslim Asians, led

Genghis Khan is shown receiving the spoils of battle after conquering many Muslim peoples.

by the world conqueror Genghis Khan. The Mongol invasion seemed like an unexplainable natural disaster to the Iranian and other Muslim peoples in their path. Cities were burned to the ground, untold thousands were massacred, and towers of human skulls were piled up along the roads as a warning to those who refused to submit. Even worse, the Mongols had no use for agriculture, and, along with cities, destroyed the irrigation system that had made farming possible in the dry lands of the Middle East.

In 1258, the Mongol invaders captured and sacked Baghdad, murdering the ruling caliph. A century later another central Asian tribe, the Tartars, swept across Iran and devastated the land. But ultimately the resilience of its people enabled Iranian society to survive. Mongols and Tartars settled down, were converted to Islam, and became peaceful farmers and herdsmen as their descendants are today, another part of the ethnic mosaic of Iran.

Forming a Shia Nation

The final building block in the construction of a separate Islamic nation in Iran was put in place in the early sixteenth century. At that time the country was controlled by various local rulers. A brotherhood of dervishes (from the Farsi word *darwish*, meaning "poor"), the Islamic counterpart of Christian monks, had established their headquarters in the northwest. The order took its name from that of its founder, Safa, just as Christian orders like the Benedictines and Franciscans did.

The Safavids, as they are known in history, gradually built up a powerful organization of warrior monks, expanding their territory to control a large part of northwestern Iran. In 1501 their young leader, Ismail, called a special meeting of the brotherhood. He said that he was descended from Ali and should therefore be respected as the true spiritual leader of all Shia Muslims. If they would follow him and believe in him as the agent of Ali, he would make all Iran into a mighty Shia nation, a bulwark of protection for Shias against the Sunni majority.

Ismail (ISS-may-ill) must have been an extraordinary leader since he was only sixteen when he made these statements! But he kept his word. Within a short time the Safavid order had unified all Iran. Ismail then had himself crowned by the *ulema* (religious leaders) as Shah Ismail, the first in a line of Safavid rulers in the country.

Shah Ismail then announced that Shia Islam would be the official state religion of Iran. He invited Shia Muslims from other areas of the Islamic world to come and live in safety in his land.

In this way Iran began a new way of life as a separate Islamic nation and society within the larger Islamic world, ruled by Shia monarchs and obedient to Shia belief in the line of Shia Imams descended from Ali as their spiritual leaders. The Safavid kingdom was considerably larger than present-day Iran and included Afghanistan, the Caucasus mountain region, and a large part of Iraq.

More important than territory in terms of Iran's relations with other nations was the establishment of a special relationship between the Shahs and the religious leaders (*ulema*, in Arabic, *mullahs* and *mujtahids*, or learned scholars, in Farsi), which interlocked religion and politics. When the Shahs were weak and ineffective, the mullahs functioned as a "state within a state," independent of royal authority. Conversely, when the Shahs were strong, they controlled the mullahs. In this way a stable, if uneasy, balance was established between the monarchy and religious leaders that lasted until the 1979 revolution.

Shia Iran reached another high point in the long history of Iran during the reign of Shah Abbas I (1587–1629), a contemporary of Queen Elizabeth I of England. At a time when English settlers were landing at Plymouth and Jamestown to lay the foundations for a new American nation, visitors to Shah Abbas's court in Isfahan, his capital, marveled at its magnificent mosques (Islamic houses of worship), its gardens and

Shah Abbas I ruled Iran during a high point in its history.

palaces, and its bazaar filled with priceless carpets, jewelry, copperware, and miniature paintings. To see Isfahan, according to a Persian proverb, was to see half the world!

Shah Abbas's successors were less able than he, and as a result the *ulema* controlled the population because of their role as interpreters and guides for Shia Islam. Nomadic and seminomadic tribes such as the Qashqai and the Bakhtiyari declared their independence, and to make matters worse, European countries, notably Great Britain, France, and Russia, sought control of Iran for its strategic location and resources. By the mid-nineteenth century, as these countries prepared to divide the realm of Cyrus into colonies and protectorates, the Shah scanned the horizon in a desperate effort to find allies that might help him stave off occupation. As he did so, his choice fell on the United States, an unknown faraway nation not likely to be interested in Iran's resources or its territory.

Chapter II A Century of Friendship

In the late 1700s a new line of Shahs, the Qajars, seized power in Iran. They established control through violent methods; thus the first Qajar Shah put out the eyes of some 20,000 residents of the city of Kerman because it had backed his chief rival. Elimination of rivals and the establishment of absolute power for monarchs assured long reigns for several Shahs, notably Nasir al-Din Shah (1848–1896), a contemporary of Queen Victoria of England.

Left alone, Iran would probably have limped along indefinitely with little change in the lives of its people. However, the great changes in Europe brought about by the Industrial Revolution and the resulting demand for raw materials made Iran a logical target because of its important natural resources, notably petroleum. Russia, its nearest European neighbor, was the first to move in. Despite the Shah's boast that his armies were "as numerous as the stars," they proved inferior to Russian forces and were routed in two wars, 1818 and 1826–1828. The second war ended with the Treaty of Turkomanchai, which took away considerable Iranian territory and saddled the Shah's regime with heavy war costs.

Iran was saved at this critical time in its history only by the intervention of Great Britain. Both Great Britain and Russia wanted to control the country; Britain in order to protect its sea-trade routes through the Indian Ocean to India, Russia in order to reach its goals of a land empire in Asia and access to all-weather, ice-free ports for its southern trade. Neither country would allow the other a free hand in Iran. As a result, Iran's location between the territories of two more powerful countries saved it from being gobbled up by one or the other.

First U.S. Contact

A basic principle of American foreign policy as it developed after independence was *isolation*—staying out of the conflicts and rivalries of other nations, especially those of Europe. With one or two exceptions, U.S. presidents from George Washington to Woodrow Wilson held firmly to this principle. However, private American institutions, notably churches, became concerned early on with the plight of Christian populations living under non-Christian rule in other parts of the world, especially the Middle East. Most of this region was ruled at that time by the Muslim Ottoman Turks. Under their rule, and in accordance with Islamic law, Christians and Jews were "protected" peoples. They were exempt from military service and were allowed to practice their religious rites and customs without interference. They had to pay a special tax in return for this protection, and were treated as inferior peoples by the Muslim majority. American pilgrims to the Holy Land of Palestine brought back horror stories about the poverty and lack of medical and educational services available to Christians living there, and urged their churches to "do something" to help these forgotten Christian communities.

The situation for the Christian population of Iran was, if anything, worse than it was in Palestine. This was due in large measure to Iran's political instability. Although the Qajars were in theory absolute rulers, in practice they used a "divide and rule" policy to stay in power, encouraging tribal, ethnic, and religious conflicts. The Christians, being the smallest and politically weakest of Iran's various population groups, suffered the most at the hands of rampaging Muslim mobs.

Thus the first involvement of the United States in Iran grew out of humanitarian concerns. In 1834 the Board of Foreign Missions of the Presbyterian Church (United States) sent out missionaries to set up a school in Urumiya (modern Rezaiyeh) in Azerbaijan province for Christian children living there. The school had a typical American curriculum with such subjects as history, geography, arithmetic, biology, and geometry, along with Bible study. These subjects were utterly unknown to Iranian children at that time, both Muslims and non-Muslims. The only schools in Iran then were the few Islamic primary schools where Muslim boys (but not girls) were taught to recite the Koran until they could do so perfectly. About 99 percent of the population could neither read nor write in their own language, and there were no schools or teachers in the Christian communities.

It is not surprising, therefore, that when the first missionaries arrived in Urumiya they were greeted with a parade of Christian youngsters beating drums and clashing cymbals! In the years that followed, American missionaries set up schools until there were

Girls line up for a photograph outside their school in the 1880s.

This school in Tehran was run by Presbyterian missionaries.

more than forty in Iran. These schools were intended to serve the small Christian and Zoroastrian population, but they had a spin-off effect on the Muslims. In 1840 the Shah opened the first school for Muslim children with a Western curriculum, the *Dar al-Fonun* ("House of Sciences") in Tehran. It was modeled on the Christian mission schools, with European teachers and a curriculum of familiar subjects. The first school for girls was established in 1874; its pupils included Christians, Jews, and Muslims, with school fees for the latter paid by the government.

As more young Iranians were exposed to Western ideas through these schools and through studies in Europe, they became aware of the weaknesses of the Iranian political system. They also observed the ignorance of other cultures and political and social systems of the *ulema*. The constant rivalry for power between the Shah and religious leaders seemed to them to be a major obstacle to Iran's development as a nation.

Gradually these young Iranians began to think in terms of placing limits on the absolute power of Shahs and trade-offs between rulers and *ulema*. This movement toward constitutional government to replace absolute rule began in Azerbaijan, the Turkish-speaking westernmost province of Iran. The first American mission school had been established there, and many young Azerbaijanis had traveled and studied in Europe. The idea that caught their attention was that of government by a *constitution*, a man-made instrument that would set limits on the absolute power of a ruler. A constitution would also allow elected institutions (like the British Parliament and the United States Congress) to share in the responsibilities of government.

Gradually an organized Movement for a Constitution in Iran came into existence. In the beginning its membership was small, limited to educated young Azerbaijanis. But before long it would grow into a mighty flood that would sweep all Iranians along in mass opposition to the monarchy.

Ironically, Nasir al-Din Shah helped the cause of the constitutional movement by his own actions. By sending young Iranians to Europe to study, he enabled them to see with their own eyes the difference between their undeveloped society and the industrially advanced societies of Europe. The Shah also gave out contracts to foreign companies to develop and market Iran's natural resources. The idea behind these "concessions" was that their development would bring revenues into Iran and enable the country to build up its economy. Unfortunately many of the concessions were granted to unscrupulous foreigners, helped by dishonest Iranian court officials, who siphoned off most of the revenues. In this way the funds needed to make Iran into a modern country on the European model simply disappeared.

By 1891, Iran was almost bankrupt. Its income from concessions and foreign bank loans was used up in bribes to court officials, mismanagement, and profiteering. In order to make interest payments on the loans, the Shah gave a fifty-year monopoly over the production and sale of tobacco to an English company. This concession aroused a storm of protest. Not only were (and are) Iranians heavy smokers, but also the prospect of having to pay inflated prices for their own tobacco seemed an insult to national pride. The *mullahs* decreed that use of tobacco was contrary to Islamic law. Tobacco sellers closed their shops, people destroyed or hid the pipes with which they smoked, and "in a marvelously short time the use of tobacco practically ceased."[4]

Faced with nearly unanimous resistance, the Shah canceled the concession, and the water pipes reappeared. But the pressure for a constitution continued. A decade later, the situation came to a head. Outraged that they were not being heard, people poured into the streets demanding an end to foreign control over the economy and a constitution that would limit the Shah's absolute power. The Shah's soldiers fired on

Nasir al-Din Shah bowed to the will of the people and established a constitution and national legislature.

the crowds, and in response, thousands of demonstrators took refuge in mosques and thousands more were allowed to camp in the vast walled grounds of the British Legation (Embassy) in Tehran. They did so, rather than engage in futile resistance, under the ancient Iranian tradition of *bast* (sanctuary). This tradition allows those who seek safety from oppression or persecution to go into public buildings, such as churches, mosques, or embassies, where they come under God's protection and may not be molested. This particular *bast* (strangely similar to the 1979 revolution) united all classes in opposition to the Shah, and national life came to a dead stop.

Faced with the opposition of all his people, Nasir al-Din Shah gave in. He approved a constitution. One of its provisions established a national legislature (Parliament, *Majlis* in the Persian language) which would be responsible for making the laws of the land. Members would be elected by the people. The first Majlis met in October 1906, and even in later years of dictatorship, it continued to function in the manner of the U.S. Congress.

An American Martyr

During the nineteenth and early twentieth centuries, American missionaries continued to work as teachers and medical doctors in Iran, building friendship and helping to educate the young Iranians in their charge and expose them to new ideas. But officially the United States took no part in the effort to develop Iran's economy. The United States did not have an embassy in the country until 1883, and none of the Shah's concessions went to American banks, companies, or individuals. However, the efforts of newly crowned Muhammad Ali Shah Qajar (1907–1909) to do away with the constitution and abolish the Majlis brought about American intervention in an unexpected way.

In 1909 the Shah sent his army to Tabriz, capital of Azerbaijan. As noted earlier, the province had been the cradle of the constitutional movement, due in part to the presence of American schools and the presence of many European-educated intellectuals. The Shah was determined to crush opposition. His troops surrounded Tabriz and planned to starve the population into surrendering.

As the siege proceeded, teachers at the American Mission School became concerned about the plight of their students and their families because of a growing shortage of food and water. One of the newer teachers was a tall young man with flaming red hair and intense blue eyes named Howard Baskerville. After graduating from Princeton Seminary in New Jersey, he had come to Iran as a missionary teacher. Baskerville was very popular with his students. He had gotten to know many of them outside of class and had gained considerable knowledge of Iranian politics from them. As the siege went on he became concerned about the lack of food and water in the city. Although members of the school staff were officially forbidden to involve themselves in local politics, Baskerville was determined to help the constitutional cause in which he had come to believe with great passion.

Despite warnings from his superiors, Baskerville secretly organized his students into a militia, gave them some basic military training, and armed them with German-made, short-barreled Mauser rifles that he had stolen from the city arsenal. On a cool April evening he led them in a desperate attempt to break the siege but was shot and killed during the breakout.

Howard Baskerville was not the first American to die for the cause of freedom. But he was the first to die on Iranian soil for the cause of freedom in Iran. He was buried in Tabriz. Although his heroism and death received little notice in the U.S. press, from the Iranian viewpoint his tomb remains a symbol of the friendship of the two nations begun with the mission schools and deepened by Baskerville's martyrdom in the cause of constitutional government in Iran.

The Shuster Mission

In 1911, two years after the siege of Tabriz had been lifted and constitutional government reinstated throughout the country, the Majlis began a search for foreign economists who might be able to reorganize Iranian finances and bring order into its chaotic economy. Because the United States was far away and was considered a loyal but disinterested friend, the choice turned naturally to American economists. President William Howard Taft was contacted and agreed to name W. Morgan Shuster, economic adviser to the Department of State in Washington, to head a "mission" in Iran. Shuster had had previous experience developing finance and accounting systems in other countries and was considered the best qualified person for such a mission. Upon his arrival in Tehran after a two-month journey by steamship, side-wheeler, motor launch, sailboat, and finally carriage across oceans, seas, lakes, rivers, and the dusty roads of the Iranian Plateau, he and his party were welcomed by the U.S. minister and a huge crowd of Iranians curious to see these strangers from the other side of the world who had come to help them.

The Majlis appointed Shuster treasurer-general of the empire and presented him with an elegant palace in Tehran for office use; it had been the summer residence of a former prime minister. Shuster and his team set to work with typical American thoroughness and efficiency, and in a very short time they set up an

American-style tax collection system. For the first time since the reign of Shah Abbas I three centuries earlier, taxes were collected in orderly fashion in Iran.

Unfortunately, Shuster's work brought him into conflict not only with wealthy landowners and members of the Shah's court (who found themselves suddenly paying taxes for the first time) but also with the Russians. The latter still controlled much of northern Iran, and they not only refused entry to the treasurer-general but also blocked efforts by his tax collectors to carry out their work.

Shuster's failure was also to play an "American" game, assuming goodwill on everyone's part and failing to build a support base among the Iranians with whom he was working. Nine months after his arrival the Russian government sent a *demarche* (official demand) to the Iranian government ordering his dismissal. Russian troops marched on Tehran to back the demand. Lacking support from either those who had hired him or his own government—the Department of State, his original employer, had advised him that he was on his own, with no official U.S. connection—the treasurer-general had no choice but to resign. He returned home to write an account of his experience, *The Strangling of Persia*, leaving behind continued goodwill toward Americans but little of a practical nature other than the skeleton structure of a workable accounting and tax system.

Iran and World War I

When World War I broke out in 1914, Iran declared its neutrality. However, Great Britain and Russia, who were allied against Germany, suspected, with some justification, that German agents were using the country for espionage and a possible end-run attack against Russia. British and Russian armies occupied Iran and divided it into two occupation zones, with a neutral zone under Iranian government control around Tehran. As the war went on, the end of Iranian independence seemed closer than ever.

Once again the country was saved, when the Russian government of the czar was overthrown in 1917 by a revolution. The government of the new Soviet Union signed a treaty with Iran in 1921 in which it canceled all Iranian debts to the czar's government and renounced all claims to Iranian territory. British occupation forces had already left, so for the first time in a century Iran was free from all forms of foreign control.

Although its sovereignty had been restored, the country's internal political situation remained unstable. Communists in Gilan province, with the backing of the new Soviet government, declared an independent Republic of Gilan there. The Kurds also refused to accept the authority of the central government. Iran's nomadic tribes, traditionally independent, continued to follow their age-old wandering lifestyle, paying no taxes and obeying no laws other than their tribal ones.

New Hero, New Dynasty

At this pivotal point in the country's national history a new hero appeared to save Iran, riding out of the mist like a modern-day Rustam.

His original name was simply Reza. He was born in 1878 in Alasht, a tiny village of stone houses with thatched roofs clinging to a mountainside in the province of Mazanderan, southwest of the Caspian

> The exploits of Rustam, Iran's mythical hero who rescued kings long ago and saved the nation on many occasions, are told at length in the *Shahnameh* (Book of Kings), the national epic. It was written more than a thousand years ago, but Iranians still learn its tales as children and can recite them from memory.

Sea. He was orphaned at an early age and brought up by his mother's brother. The uncle was a military man, so when Reza was fifteen he was enrolled in the Cossack Brigade, a special unit in the Iranian Army commanded and trained by Russian officers. Reza showed military skills and leadership ability early on. These skills plus his height (he was more than six feet) enabled him to move up through the ranks of the Brigade. By the end of World War I he had become a colonel and commander of a division.

His military prestige, along with command of reliable troops, gave Reza Khan (his new official title) a power base from which to launch a political career. The springboard to power was through military success. Reza directed successful operations against the Kurds and the nomadic tribes, forcing them to accept central government authority. The Communist Republic of Gilan collapsed after Soviet troops there withdrew under the terms of the 1921 treaty, and Iran again became a unified country. From then on the star of this Mazanderan farmer's son rose rapidly. The Majlis appointed him minister of war and then prime minister. And in 1925, with the last Qajar Shah, Ahmad, in comfortable exile, Reza Khan was crowned as Shahinshah Reza Pahlavi, founder of a new

Reza Khan started his public life in the military, quickly rising through its ranks and becoming minister of war, then prime minister, and finally, Reza Shah.

dynasty and latest in a two-thousand-year parade of monarchs in Iran.

Under Reza Shah, Iran entered a new phase in its long and storied history. The Shah was a great admirer of Mustafa Kemal Ataturk, a military leader who had established the new Republic of Turkey on the ruins of the defeated Ottoman Empire and was working to transform Turkish society into a modern one along European lines. Reza Shah aspired to do the same for Iranian society. He was determined to bring Iran into the modern world and be recognized as a modern nation. To do so he would break the power of the *mullahs* over the people and eliminate outdated customs and traditions based on Islam that he felt were partially responsible for his people's backwardness. He would also lay the base for a modern economy, building roads, industries, and railroads, form a well-equipped army, and restore national pride. And he would do all this with as little help as possible from other countries, so that Iran would emerge free and proud from its backward condition.

In making these sweeping changes, and particularly those involving social behavior and customs, Reza Shah ruled as an absolute monarch in the manner of Shahs of old. He kept the forms and institutions of constitutional government, but issued new laws in the form of decrees, which were automatically approved by the Majlis under a rubber-stamp process. Thus, in order to break the power of religious leaders over the people, he confiscated all lands and properties held in trust by them to manage on behalf of the community of Islam. Other decrees forbade women to wear veils or the *chador* (a full-length robe that covered them from head to toe except for the eyes) when they went out in public. Men were ordered to wear hats or caps with brims instead of the traditional tall, conical, brimless fez. These restrictions may seem ridiculous or an infringement on individual rights to us today, but Reza Shah said that such articles of clothing were examples of the heavy hand of Islam that lay oppressively on his people and kept them from becoming a modern society.

The First Millspaugh Mission

Reza Shah had managed to rid Iran of foreign occupation, but the country was still in very bad shape financially. And remembering earlier U.S. assistance, he turned again to the United States for help. Due to Shuster's work the United States continued to be viewed in Iran as a disinterested friend. Thus in 1922, prior to Reza's accession to the throne, the Majlis asked the U.S. Department of State to send out a second economic mission. This one would be headed by Dr. Arthur Millspaugh, Shuster's successor as economic adviser to the department. Millspaugh was given the title treasurer-general like his predecessor, and in this capacity was responsible for all aspects of Iran's finances, from tax collection and budgets to disbursements. As he wrote in his memoirs: "We applied the law courteously but without favoritism. We said no in kind tones but with monotonous regularity and occasionally with emphasis. The Persians [sic] nicknamed me Dr. Poul Nist, 'Dr. There is no money!'"[5]

By 1926 the Millspaugh mission had accomplished most of its goals. It had balanced the budget, set up regular accounting procedures, and reestablished orderly tax collections. Wealthy landowners and high-ranking government officials who had never paid taxes because they felt it was beneath their dignity to do so suddenly found themselves being dunned for back obligations. New taxes on tea, tobacco, matches, and sugar helped pay for new roads, schools, hospitals, and the Trans-

Iranian Railroad, an engineering marvel that spanned the country from north to south and was Reza Shah's proudest achievement, mainly because it had been paid for entirely without foreign loans!

But Millspaugh's successes carried a high price. Wealthy landowners and government officials were angered by the taxes, while the poor groaned over having to pay more for the things they could not live without. What ultimately brought the Millspaugh mission to an abrupt end was a change in attitude on the part of Reza Shah. As prime minister he had asked for such a mission and welcomed its arrival. But after he became Shah his strong commitment to Iranian nationalism led him to adopt extremely antiforeign views. He was determined to lift Iran out of poverty and backwardness by its own efforts, with minimal help from the outside world. From his perspective even the help of the United States as a disinterested friend was suspect. In this respect he was very different from his son, who many years later would become so closely identified with American aid that to his own people he seemed to have become a U.S. puppet.

End of an Era

When World War II broke out in 1939, Reza Shah declared that Iran would stay neutral. Unfortunately, the British and French, allies against Nazi Germany, suspected that he was secretly pro-German. There seemed to be some truth to their suspicions, because in the 1930s the Shah had invited German advisers to help set up factories for the use of his country's resources. British suspicions deepened after Germany had invaded the Soviet Union in 1941 and Britain had automatically become its ally. Fearing that Iran was about to become a German base for a second front against the Soviet Union, British and Soviet troops jointly occupied the country in August 1941. The Shah said sadly, "Our friends and Russia are giving us the same treatment that Hitler gave to Belgium and Mussolini gave to Greece."[6] Wishing only to save his throne, he abdicated in favor of his twenty-one-year-old son, Muhammad Reza. Reza Shah was taken aboard a British warship to South Africa, where he died in 1944, ostensibly from cardiac arrest but in reality from a broken heart; he had simply lost the will to live. He had reigned for sixteen years and brought about great changes not only in Iran's economy but also (at least superficially) in the attitudes and values of its society.

Ironically the Anglo-Soviet occupation brought about a much closer relationship between Iran and the United States than would have been possible in Reza Shah's time. Prior to the occupation the Shah had sent a cable to President Franklin D. Roosevelt asking him to use his "good offices" as a friend to Iran to intercede with the British and Soviet governments. Roosevelt's reply merely assured the Shah that those two countries had no designs on Iranian independence. The United States had not yet entered the war, and Roosevelt accepted at face value British Prime Minister Winston Churchill's argument that Iran's strategic location made it an essential supply route for assistance to the hard-pressed Soviet Union. From 1943, however, some 30,000 American nonmilitary personnel poured into Iran to keep the route open for a steady stream of military supplies to the Soviet Union. And in this indirect way Iran became a key player in the "game" of international politics, this time more closely aligned in a political way with the United States.

Chapter III Front Line of the Cold War

R eza Shah's abdication and exile brought to the throne a twenty-one-year-old youth with no experience in government and very little training in leadership. The crown prince had been a sickly child and nearly died of typhoid fever when he was seven. His father set up a special elementary school in the palace for him and a few other sons of aristocratic families, and in 1931, when he was eleven, sent him to a private boarding school in Switzerland for further studies. There he learned French and how to fly a small airplane, a skill that would prove valuable to him in later years. He also became familiar with European culture, which seemed to him superior in some ways to his own Iranian way of life. In this respect he was very different from his father, who left Iran only once (to visit Turkey) and remained a sincere patriot all his life.

Muhammed Reza returned to Iran in 1936, and his father enrolled him in the Tehran military academy, the Iranian equivalent of West Point. The training was very tough, and due to his son's position as Iran's future king, Reza Shah insisted that he be treated with stricter discipline than his classmates. As a result, the crown prince developed a fascination with military matters that carried over into his rule when he became Shah. At the same time, he formed friendships with classmates who would later become senior army officers, thus ensuring army loyalty and support during his reign.

Other than a brief daily lunch with his son, Reza Shah had given him little information about his future role and responsibilities. When Muhammed Reza was suddenly placed on the throne, he had to depend upon his father's advisers for guidance. His own personality was another obstacle to leadership. He had grown up under a strong-willed father and an equally forceful twin sister, and he was by nature cautious and indecisive. In his heart he wanted to be a strong leader in the mold of Reza Shah, but he did not know how to do so.

Iran's wartime situation was a second major obstacle for the new Shah. After the German invasion of the Soviet Union, British and Soviet forces jointly occupied Iran to keep it from becoming a German base. A 1942 Anglo-Soviet treaty committed both occupying powers to respect Iran's independence and withdraw their troops within six months of the end of the war.

The United States Enters Iran

Except for the few missionaries who went to Iran in the 1800s, the country was a remote and unknown place for most Americans until World War II. They would have been hard pressed to find it on a global map. For U.S. Foreign Service officers assigned to the American consulate (later embassy) in Tehran it was a thankless assignment with few attractions. They were not fluent in Farsi, the spoken language, and knew little of Iranian customs and culture. This lack of understanding led to a tragic incident in the 1920s. A newly arrived American vice-consul, Andrew Imbrie, was attacked and killed by an enraged mob while taking photographs of women washing in a sacred fountain adjoining a local mosque. The scene made a superb picture in his viewfinder, but it was a deep offense to Iranian Islamic customs.

The U.S. entry into World War II resulted in the first large-scale involvement of Americans in Iran. U.S. military strategists were concerned with finding a safe route for sending military equipment and supplies to the Soviet Union (USSR), which had become a U.S. ally in the war with Germany. The shortest practical route for such supplies was through Iran. The War Department (now the Department of Defense) set up the Persian Gulf Command (PGC) in 1942 to take charge of the Iranian transportation system and convert it to military use.

During the next two years of the war some 30,000 Americans, both military and civilian personnel, worked for the PGC in Iran. They repaired the Trans-Iranian Railroad, now deteriorated into a weed-covered single track. They set up entire truck and tank assembly plants, hired and trained hundreds of Iranian workmen, and shipped enough war equipment to Soviet armies over Iran's dusty roads and the railroad to save the Soviet Union from almost certain defeat. Through their efforts the men of the PGC strengthened and deepened the bonds of Iranian-American friendship begun a century earlier by American missionaries.[7]

"Cold War" Advisers

As an outgrowth of the PGC and the changing postwar relationship with the Soviet Union, the United States began sending advisers to Iran. The idea was that these advisers not only would train Iranians in government management and operations to help them become more efficient, but also would help Iran to become a politically stable country and therefore a valuable U.S. ally.

Unfortunately, these advisers knew little about Iran and its people, their customs, language, and ancient traditions. They assumed that the same process that had made the United States into a great nation would work automatically if transferred to Iran. They did not understand Iranian national pride and resentment of foreigners based on long and bitter historical experience.

The only one of these early American advisers who was relatively successful in his work was Colonel Norman Schwartzkopf, commander of the New Jersey State Police. Colonel Schwartzkopf had been given the apparently hopeless task of organizing Iran's 20,000-member rural police force, called a *gendarmerie* after the French term, into an effective unit. He succeeded despite the opposition of the Shah's own government officials, criticism of his work in the Iranian newspapers, and an almost total lack of U.S. government support. The measure of his success was made clear on the Shah's twenty-fifth birthday in 1944, when the former ragtag force marched proudly through Tehran in their new uniforms to celebrate the occasion.

A New Millspaugh Mission

After World War II ended, Dr. Arthur Millspaugh was invited to return to Iran to deal once again with Iran's chaotic finances. The war years and occupation by foreign troops had been hard on the country's economy. There were serious food shortages, the tax-collection system Millspaugh had set up on his first visit had not been put into effect, and money was in short supply. Millspaugh was again given the title treasurer-general and immediately went to work.

The conditions that had made Millspaugh's first mission relatively successful were no longer in effect. Iran was now ruled by a weak and inexperienced Shah, vastly different from his father in personality and leadership qualities. Soviet occupation forces in the northern region not only interfered with his work, but also diverted food supplies to send northward to nearby areas of their own country that were suffering from famine, causing food shortages in that part of Iran.

Opposition to Millspaugh increased dramatically when the treasurer-general presented his recommendations to the Majlis (his official employer, although he had been sent under U.S. government direction). The recommendations would establish a government monopoly over production and sale of wheat, a basic part of the Iranian diet. Other recommendations included an income tax on the wealthy and salary cuts for the huge number of government employees, most of whom did little or no work but held their jobs because they were related to someone.

Millspaugh's recommendations made good sense financially, and if adopted they would probably put Iran back on a sound economic basis. But they pleased almost none of the groups in Iranian society. The wealthy landowners objected to the income tax, and government employees blocked the entrances to the Majlis building to protest the proposed salary cuts. The treasurer-general also had personality problems. He offended many of the officials he dealt with by his high-handed manner and his refusal to compromise with what he called the "classes of selfish privilege." He also showed a lack of judgment. Thus he supported a bill by one group of Majlis deputies that would cut the size and expense of the army, saying that it was "this wasteful government's most colossal extravagance."[8] While the statement was true, other deputies accused him with some justification of interfering in the country's internal affairs. After the Majlis had called for his resignation several times and his own government refused to support him, he resigned abruptly with his work only partly finished. His final words seem prophetic:

> Some time soon the American and British governments must decide whether Soviet cooperation is available on terms compatible with a peaceful world order. Moscow appears to have accepted division of the world into two power blocs. If the United States and Britain decide likewise they must draw a line around the Soviet world and take their stand in defense of that line. Whether Persia [sic] should be on one side or the other or half on one side and half on the other must also be decided.[9]

Crisis in Azerbaijan, 1946

Millspaugh's "prophecy" was proven in the months following the end of the war. Wartime cooperation between the United States, its allies, and the Soviet Union broke down over a number of issues involving areas under German or Japanese occupation or located next to Soviet territory. These included Poland, other countries in Eastern Europe, and the Balkans, Korea, Manchuria in northeast China, and Iran. It would not be fair to say that the Cold War began in Iran. But of all

> The Kurds, who are believed by many scholars to be descended from the ancient Medes, have fought for centuries for a nation of their own, but have never had one because of international rivalries and power politics. Today they are ruled separately by the governments of Iran, Iraq, Syria, and Turkey, forming an important minority in each country.

these issues, the Iranian one came on the heels of the wartime alliance and seemed to prove to U.S. leaders that the Soviet Union was bent on domination of Europe and eventually the entire world.

The pattern of events in Iran supported this belief. Britain and the USSR had agreed in their 1942 treaty that all occupation forces would be withdrawn from Iran within six months of the end of the war. The United States had already closed down the Persian Gulf Command, and British forces met the withdrawal deadline. The Soviet Union, however, not only kept its occupation forces in place but also supported efforts by non-Iranian minorities such as Azeris and Kurds to declare their independence from the Iranian central government.

The Azeris, the largest population group in the province, had some legitimate grievances. They had led the constitutional movement, but Reza Shah had reimposed absolute rule after he became Shah, and he ignored the constitution. They were not allowed to collect local and provincial taxes (as was their legal right). Their native Turkish language was not taught in their schools, and all official documents had to be in Farsi. These restrictions were continued by the Shah's

The "domino theory" holds that when one country falls under foreign (that is, Communist) control its neighbor countries will fall under the same control, like a row of dominoes when the first one is knocked down.

advisers after his abdication. Most of them had stayed on to advise his young son, and the wartime occupation by British and Soviet forces discouraged attempts at reforms.

The Soviet Union also encouraged an Azeri separatist movement backed by Soviet occupation forces and under official Soviet protection. In 1945 the Democratic party of Azerbaijan was organized with Soviet help. Its founder, Jafar Pishevari, had spent many years in exile in the USSR. Early in 1946, Pishevari presented the Shah with three demands: use of Azeri Turkish as the official language of the province, devotion of all tax revenues collected there for provincial economic development, and establishment of a provincial legislature as had been specified in the original (1906) Iranian constitution. If these demands were not met, Pishevari threatened, Azerbaijan would "fight to the death" for its freedom.

At the same time that Azerbaijan was threatening to break away, Kurdish leaders in northwest Iran announced the formation of an independent Kurdish Republic of Mahabad (named for its capital).

With the separation of Azerbaijan and Kurdistan it seemed very likely that Iran soon would no longer exist as an independent nation in its own territory. The first stage would be the incorporation of Azerbaijan into the

Soviet Union as a new Soviet "republic." But the report that Communists were in control of the province set alarm bells ringing in Washington. American foreign-policy leaders feared that the fall of Iran, or part of it, into the Soviet orbit would be followed by the Sovietization of other Middle Eastern countries, one by one, until that entire strategic region was in Soviet hands.

At first the U.S. response to what were seen as Soviet provocations in Azerbaijan was limited to protests to the Soviet government from the American Embassy in Moscow. But officials in the Department of State who had had first-hand experience in Iran were convinced that control of Azerbaijan was a first step toward a Soviet takeover of all of Iran. As a result, they developed what would be called later the "containment" policy. It had four objectives: (1) to stop Soviet expansion by all means short of war; (2) to guarantee Iran's independence; (3) to strengthen the newly formed United Nations (UN) as a preserver of world peace; and (4) to protect vital American interests (particularly the oil industry in the Middle East). Support for Iran against Soviet penetration was seen as essential for reaching these objectives.

The UN and the Azerbaijan Crisis

The shutdown of the Persian Gulf Command had left no American forces in Iran, and the withdrawal of British troops meant that no foreign military forces were available to counter the Soviet threat to Azerbaijan. The Iranian Army lacked the manpower and equipment needed to restore government control over the province. In any case, President Harry S. Truman had ruled out military intervention. American troops were coming home from war, not returning to fight a new one.

However, the United Nations provided a platform from which actions such as the Soviet "occupation" of Azerbaijan could be criticized publicly as a threat to world peace. Iran's UN representative presented a complaint to the Security Council charging the Soviet Union with interference in Iranian internal affairs and demanding the withdrawal of Soviet occupation forces.

The Iranian complaint was one of the first to be presented to the Security Council, which is the organization within the UN charged with responsibility for world peace. And because the complaint involved the Soviet Union, one of the five permanent members of the council, it loomed as a test case of the UN's ability to maintain world peace and resolve disputes between member states without the use of force.

In retrospect, the significance of the Azerbaijan crisis, which had occupied world attention, seems to have been the exposure to international criticism of a somewhat crude attempt by the Soviet Union to take over a neighboring country. The UN Charter gives each Security Council member the power to veto any actions taken by the council that it feels would affect its own national interests. However, the USSR not only did not use its veto power, it also agreed to negotiate directly with Iran on the matter of troop withdrawal. Under a new agreement the withdrawal would be completed within six weeks. In return the Soviets would be given the right to search for oil in northern Iran, an area outside the concession area controlled by the British-owned Anglo-Iranian Oil Company, manager of Iran's oil industry. The Soviet Union kept its part of the agreement, and in November 1946,

Iranian government troops entered Azerbaijan and put a quick end to the democratic "republic" established there months earlier.

The Azerbaijan crisis is a good example of the difficulties often faced by powerful nations in dealing with small but strategically important nations without the use of military force. In the Iranian case, a law passed by the Majlis in 1944 required its approval for all foreign concession grants for development of natural resources, specifically oil, before they could go into effect. In 1946 the agreement to allow Soviet oil exploration in northern Iran was presented to the Majlis for the necessary approval and was promptly rejected. Having withdrawn its occupation forces, the USSR had no means other than invasion to force Iran to keep its part of the agreement. Consequently, the Soviet Union lost face and leverage. The United States in contrast now became Iran's major ally in the emerging Cold War, and it had done so without military intervention or financial cost.

Chapter IV Oil and Turmoil

The strong backing of the United States and the success of the Iranian army in restoring government authority in Azerbaijan and Kurdistan helped to boost the young Shah's confidence in his ability to lead his people. An unsuccessful assassination attempt in 1949 ironically increased his self-confidence; he began to believe he had the special protection of God and was destined to do great things.[10] As a result of this new belief and confidence, he formed in his mind a "grand design" that would make Iran economically strong and capable of resisting foreign invasions.

The Shah's grand design included an army equipped with the latest weapons and an economic development program that would bring Iran up to the level of the nations of Europe. Much of it would be financed by oil revenues, but it would still require large amounts of American aid money. Late in 1949 the Shah went to Washington, D.C., hat in hand, confident he would get what was needed.

By that time U.S. foreign policy was moving in a different direction. From the president on down, U.S.

leaders were preoccupied with the likelihood of the fall of China to the Communist army of Mao Tse-tung. Containment of the Soviet Union had become a secondary issue. The greatest threat to world peace, in the U.S. view, was an aggressive Communist China rather than a weakened Soviet Union. The Shah went home empty-handed, flattered as a head of state but given neither money nor specific promises of aid.

Oil Nationalization

Oil (crude petroleum) was first discovered underground in Iran in 1907, although nomadic tribesmen had used it for centuries from pools on the ground to light their cooking fires. Under the terms of the original concession a British company, the Anglo-Iranian Oil Company (AIOC), was formed to produce, refine, and export Iranian oil to foreign markets. Oil became an important fuel for industrial nations around the time of World War I, and with the advent of the automobile in the twentieth century was essential to European and American development.

The concession agreement gave Iran a very small percentage of AIOC oil sales in the form of royalty payments per barrel sold. After Reza Shah came to power he said this arrangement was an insult to Iran, and in 1933 he threw the original agreement into the fireplace of the royal palace and demanded a new one with royalties of 30 percent.[11] After much hard bargaining the company agreed to 8 percent royalty payments in return for an extension of its concession to 1993 (sixty years).

At that time Iran was in no position to push for higher royalties since it lacked the technicians to run the industry or the shops and refinery facilities to market its oil. But after World War II and the recovery of control over its own territory, Iranian negotiators made repeated efforts to negotiate a new contract with higher payments. In 1949, AIOC offered a 16 percent royalty increase but refused a number of Iranian demands that would have gone along with the increase.[12]

Feelings about foreign control were running high in Iran at that time, particularly in the Majlis. As a result, acting under the same 1944 law that had been used to annul the Soviet oil concession, the deputies voted to cancel the 1933 agreement. Henceforth Iran's oil industry from well to refinery to tanker would belong *exclusively* to the country. It would be *nationalized*, that is, controlled and managed by the nation rather than a private foreign-owned oil company.

The Pajama Man

The movement to take control of Iran's own oil industry was led by a member of the Majlis, little known outside his country, who would shortly become a familiar figure for Americans, famous for his pajamas, his weeping fits, and other peculiar behavior that masked a razor-sharp mind and strong-willed patriotism. In the 1970s and 1980s, Shah Mohammed Reza Pahlavi and the Ayatollah Khomeini were the two Iranian leaders who personified the relationship between the United States and Iran and the change from ally to enemy that came as a result of their actions and personalities. But in the 1950s, Mohammed Mossadegh had a similar impact on the relationship.

Who was this man who was able to challenge a big oil company and an even bigger United States in the

Mohammed Mossadegh opposed Reza Shah even as
prime minister under the Shah. This photograph was
taken after Mossadegh was driven from his Tehran home
by mobs who wanted to keep the Shah in power.

name of his country? By the time Mossadegh came to
international notice he was already in his sixties, with
a long career in politics and government service
behind him. Born into a wealthy landowning family
in the last years of the Qajar monarchy, he had been
appointed tax collector in his native province at the

age of fourteen! In the years that followed he took an active part in the 1905–1906 constitutional movement, studied law in Switzerland, and was the first Iranian to earn a Ph.D. (in law) from a European university. Upon his return he was elected to the Majlis for the first of many terms. Although he was himself a wealthy landowner, he was also a sincere patriot and defender of what he believed were his country's best interests, the two major ones being Iranian control over its own territory and resources and constitutional government.

During his years in politics, Mossadegh opposed Reza Shah, saying that the Shah had gained power only through the help of the British. Mossadegh opposed the Millspaugh mission on the grounds that its members were incompetent and that Millspaugh's dictatorial authority over the economy violated the constitution. And after World War II he became concerned about the greatly increased American involvement in Iran, which he feared would restore foreign control. The consistency of his position won him great popularity with the Iranian people.

In 1944, as chairman of the Majlis oil committee, Mossadegh was responsible for the law requiring Majlis approval of all foreign concessions involving Iran's natural resources. This position caused him to take a leading role in the cancellation of the 1933 oil agreement. But Iranian determination to control its oil production and exports was viewed in Washington as more of a threat to U.S. interests in the Middle East than as an expression of legitimate national rights. The outbreak of the Korean War caused fear of a worldwide oil shortage, and U.S. leaders considered it important that Iranian oil continue flowing to Western

Europe and America. To ensure this, they urged Muhammad Reza Shah in strong terms to appoint a prime minister who could work out a compromise agreement with the AIOC.

In 1950 the Shah appointed General Ali Razmara to the position. Razmara had commanded the Iranian forces that recaptured Azerbaijan, and he was considered a tough, no-nonsense soldier. Unfortunately, he had U.S. backing, which proved to be literally the kiss

General Ali Razmara (center) was

appointed prime minister in 1950.

of death for him. Many Iranians thought of him as a tool of American foreign policy. In March 1951 he was assassinated by a member of the *Fedayin-e-Islam* (Fighters for Islam), a secret organization committed to rid Iran of foreign influences by terrorist methods.

Razmara's assassination left Mossadegh as the dominant political leader in the country, and the Shah was forced to appoint him as prime minister. The bill to nationalize the oil industry was rushed through the Majlis, AIOC shut down its operations, and oil production in Iran stopped. The last sight most of the company's remaining officials had of the country that had brought them huge profits for many years was from the deck of a British cruiser carrying them downriver to the Persian Gulf, while the Union Jack waved and a military band sadly played "Rule, Britannia!"

Man of the Year, 1951

With the nationalization of the oil industry a done deal, Mohammed Mossadegh became Iran's latest hero, a new Rustam who had appeared out of nowhere to save the nation in its hour of need and faced down its most powerful enemies. But dealing with Iranians, in the words of a U.S. diplomat, is like eating soup with a fork.[13] With the oil industry idled, the unity of the various groups that had backed the prime minister began to break down, due in part to economic difficulties but also to international pressure. The AIOC organized a worldwide boycott of Iranian oil (which had stopped flowing when the British left), while the British government threatened military action and sent warships steaming toward

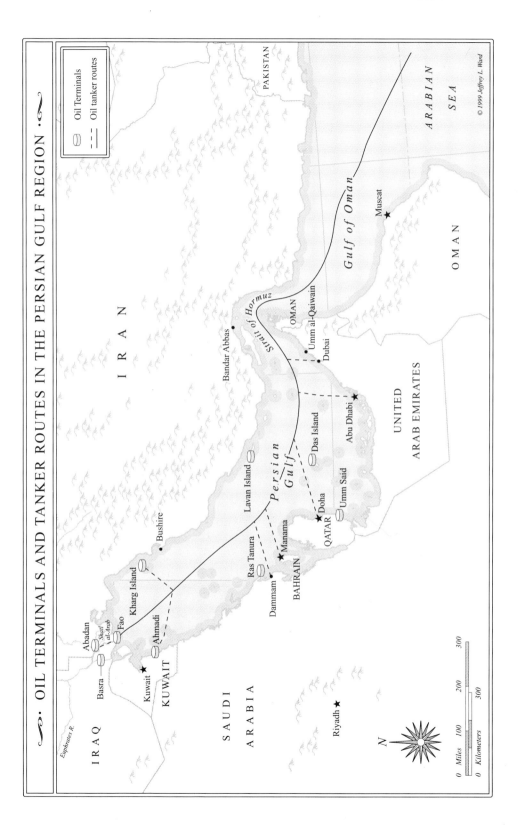

OIL TERMINALS AND TANKER ROUTES IN THE PERSIAN GULF REGION

Oil Terminals

Oil tanker routes

© 1999 Jeffrey L. Ward

IRAQ

Euphrates R.

SAUDI ARABIA

Riyadh

KUWAIT

Kuwait

Basra

Abadan

Shatt al-Arab

Fao

Ahmadi

Kharg Island

Bushire

IRAN

Ras Tanura

Dammam

BAHRAIN

Manama

QATAR

Doha

Umm Said

Lavan Island

Das Island

Abu Dhabi

UNITED ARAB EMIRATES

Bandar Abbas

Strait of Hormuz

Persian Gulf

OMAN

Umm al-Qaiwain

Dubai

OMAN

Gulf of Oman

Muscat

ARABIAN SEA

PAKISTAN

N

0   Miles   100   200   300

0   Kilometers   300

the Persian Gulf. Britain also filed a complaint with the World Court to the effect that Iran did not have a legal right to expel the AIOC. The shutdown in the oil industry brought hard times to the Iranian people. It also affected Mossadegh's popularity as the hero of nationalization. His popular support had enabled him to put together a National Front, a political organization (rather than a party, because it was made up of many different groups). Its members included bazaar merchants, university students and teachers, European-educated intellectuals, writers and journalists, and a few religious leaders. The National Front held a majority in the Majlis, and its support for Mossadegh's program of establishing a multiparty system with free elections, voting rights for women, and other features of a democratic system of government should have pleased American policy makers.

The National Front's main ally in the nationalization struggle had been the Tudeh party. It was founded in 1941 as *Hizb-e-Tudeh-e-Iran* (Party of the Iranian Masses), and from the start was Communist in its ideology and closely tied to the Soviet Union. Unlike the National Front, the Tudeh was a true political party, with a well-defined program and membership requirements. By 1950 it had 25,000 members and 300,000 supporters and was a powerful force in Iranian politics. It was the close cooperation between the Tudeh and the National Front in the nationalization struggle that concerned U.S. leaders. Many of them feared that because of its political instability and economic problems Iran was very likely to be taken over by a Communist coup, one led by the Tudeh but directed by Soviet agents.

American leaders also tended to underestimate Mossadegh and to write him off because of his unpredictable, often comic behavior. Secretary of State Dean Acheson described him as "small and frail, with not a shred of hair on his billiard-ball head . . . a long beak of a nose flanked by two bright shoe-button eyes."[14] He suffered from stomach ulcers and would often faint at the end of marathon two-day speeches in the Majlis. Due to his self-described poor health, when he became prime minister he often received official visitors lying on a hospital cot, wearing gray wool pajamas as he sipped tea with milk and saying that it was his last day on Earth. *Time* magazine named him Man of the Year for 1951. Its January 1952 cover story described him as an enigma, a fanatic, perhaps even insane. Yet more than anything else, "Old Mossy," as he was called in American newspapers and magazines, was a sincere patriot, committed to Iran's independence and control over its own territory and resources.

The Coup of 1953

The political term *coup* (*coup d'état*, in French) means the overthrow of an existing government by sudden and unexpected force, usually military. The modern history of most of the nations of Africa, Asia, and the Middle East is full of examples of such coups. But the 1953 coup in Iran was unique in two respects. First, it restored the legal ruler of the country after he had been forced out by his own government, headed by a prime minister whom he had appointed to the position. Second, the action that restored him to power was masterminded, at least initially, by agents of another government in a secret operation about which he was only marginally informed.

"Operation Ajax," as it was code-named by the handful of U.S. leaders involved in it, covered a very short period of time, from the thirtieth of the month of Tir to the twenty-eighth of Mordad (July 20–August 19, 1953). It was set in motion after Mossadegh had been given dictatorial powers by the Majlis to deal with Iran's deteriorating economy. This had come about because of the shutdown of the oil industry and the refusal of the new U.S. administration of President Dwight Eisenhower to grant emergency aid to Iran.

Using his National Front majority in the Majlis and his immense popularity as the hero of nationalization, Mossadegh issued a series of decrees that were immediately approved by the legislature. The new laws would limit the powers of the monarch and establish constitutional government, a lifetime dream of the elderly aristocrat and European-trained lawyer. They included a new electoral law with voting rights for women, health insurance and pensions for workers in industrial plants, and free education for all Iranian children through high school.

Nothing in the new laws would have offended leaders of the United States. Some years later, the Shah would incorporate them into his "White Revolution," discussed in the next chapter. But where the Shah and his U.S. backers parted company with Mossadegh was over the size of the Iranian armed forces. Mossadegh said that Iran did not need a large army equipped with the largest weapons to defend itself from attack. What the country needed, he said, was a small, well-trained police force that could keep law and order.

The Shah argued that he needed a large and powerful army as the one force he could absolutely count on to keep his throne. And the U.S. policy makers argued that it needed the Shah more than it needed Mossadegh, because he could be counted on to keep the country from going Communist. If Mossadegh were allowed to carry out his military reforms, they reasoned, the National Front/Tudeh alliance might well bring a pro-Soviet government to power in Iran, thus defeating the purpose of the *containment* policy.

It should be noted that the world situation in the 1950s looked very different than it does today. President Eisenhower had just taken office, U.S. forces were bogged down in an undeclared war in Korea, and in Indo-China (modern Vietnam, at that time a colony of France) the French Army was on the brink of being defeated by Communist guerrilla forces fighting for independence. On the U.S. home front, Senator Joseph McCarthy had built nationwide support for his efforts to root out suspected Communists in government, the arts, the press, and on university faculties. As a result, the nation was obsessed with fear of communism, not only as a hostile economic system but also as a threat to the American democratic way of life.

Operation Ajax was launched by the Central Intelligence Agency (CIA) as one of a number of undercover efforts to overthrow Communist leaders in various politically vulnerable countries. In developing the Iranian operation the CIA relied heavily on the expertise of Donald N. Wilber, an archaeologist, historian, and linguist with extensive field experience in the country and high-level contacts in its government. In his autobiography Wilber claims persuasively that he was the brains behind the operation and its chief planner.[15]

The actual implementation of Operation Ajax was entrusted to a small, ruddy-faced thirty-seven-year-old American named Kermit "Kim" Roosevelt, grandson of President Theodore Roosevelt and chief of cloak-and-dagger operations for the CIA in the Middle East. The groundwork having been laid, Roosevelt slipped across the border between Iraq and Iran and went into hiding in Tehran. Meanwhile, propaganda materials in Farsi directed against Mossadegh, including cartoons, small wall posters, and articles to be planted in the local press, had been prepared in Washington and rushed by air to Tehran, to be stored there for distribution at the proper moment.

The first step in the plan called for the Shah to dismiss Mossadegh on the grounds that he had exceeded his emergency powers. But "Old Mossy" refused to obey the Shah's order. His National Front supporters, joined by Tudeh members, took to the streets shouting "Yankee, Go Home!" (This was an angry reference to the U.S. ambassador, who seemed to them to be telling the Shah what to do.) With Mossadegh still in power and mobs roaming the streets, the Shah and his queen left the country in a two-seater airplane, flying first to Baghdad, Iraq, and then to Rome, Italy, without funds and with little more than the clothes they were wearing.

At this stage Operation Ajax began unraveling, according to its organizers in Washington. The Shah had fled—which he was not supposed to do—and key army leaders got cold feet and stayed home instead of carrying out their instructions. Mobs roamed the streets of Tehran, beating up people and tearing down statues of the Shah. As Wilber tells the story: "Decisions were taken to call off the operation. Messages to that effect reached Kim in Tehran. He ignored them, as

Muhammad Reza Shah reads the statement authorizing
a new government for his country. He was then able
to return to Iran from Rome, where he had been in exile.

the tide had begun to turn. Our propaganda material flooded Tehran, raids were mounted on Tudeh party offices and presses. Other mobs were collected from the slums of south Tehran, with ten-rial notes as incentives, and were led into the modern quarters, where they swept along soldiers and officers. General Zahedi (the Shah's choice as prime minister to replace Mossadegh) emerged from hiding to climb onto a tank and proclaim the new government.[16]

After several days of fierce street battles Mossadegh's supporters and his Tudeh allies were overcome, although the human cost was heavy, some three hundred killed and wounded. "Old Mossy" was captured as he climbed over the back fence of his residence, still in his pajamas. He was later tried by a military court and convicted of treason but was given a three-year sentence due to his health.[17] The Shah then returned to reclaim his throne, having been restored by what has been regarded ever since then, by most Iranians, as the first U.S. intervention in their internal affairs.

The success of Operation Ajax was due largely to a situation that forced the Iranian people to choose between a familiar and established government (the monarchy) and an unknown future under Mossadegh and his Tudeh allies. Given the choice, the majority chose monarchy. On the U.S. side it removed the Communist threat to Iran and ensured that the Shah, a loyal American ally, would remain in power.

Also on the positive side, the Tudeh was thoroughly purged, leaving no organized opposition to the Shah. But the U.S. intervention had its negative side as well. Its long-term effect was to alienate Iranians of all groups and social levels from their longtime friend. Many Iranians came to feel that they had finally gotten rid of one foreign power (Britain and the AIOC, its proxy) only to come under the domination of another. By the time another revolution against the Shah developed, a quarter of a century later, the majority of Iranians were strongly anti-American.

Chapter V 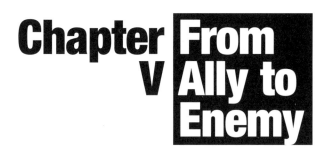From Ally to Enemy

With the Shah restored to his throne, U.S. leaders lost no time in moving to strengthen the alliance. President Eisenhower immediately granted $65.5 million in emergency aid to help the Iranian economy recover from the three-year shutdown of the oil industry. In 1954 an international consortium (group of companies) was formed to manage the industry in cooperation with the National Iranian Oil Company, established under the consortium agreement to replace AIOC. The consortium members included five U.S. oil companies, Standard of New Jersey (later Exxon), Standard of California, Mobil, Gulf, and Texaco. Later a number of small independent U.S. oil companies were allowed to buy into membership, thus securing for the United States a significant stake in Iran's huge oil market.

One important advantage to Iran of the consortium agreement was that the country would now receive 50 percent of the royalties from exports. The taps were turned on, and by 1960 Iran's oil income had soared (from $10 million in 1954) to $285 million!

The view in Washington that the Shah's regime would strongly oppose communism at home and abroad led the Eisenhower administration to provide more than $357 million in grants and loans between 1954 and 1957. In 1960 newly elected President John F. Kennedy increased this amount to $100 million a year, more than the United States gave to any country in the world that was not a member of the North Atlantic Treaty Organization (NATO).

Another important result of the overthrow of Mossadegh was a large increase in direct U.S. involvement in Iran. Not only military personnel, but technical experts from U.S. companies, foundations such as Ford and Rockefeller, and major colleges and universities, descended on Iran by the hundreds to help develop the Iranian economy through various projects. The largest project, with the U.S. company whose chief officers had developed the Tennessee Valley Authority (TVA) in the 1930s, was the development of an entire Iranian province. The province chosen was Khuzistan, a largely desert area about the size of North Carolina. The company would build a series of dams to provide water to bring unused lands under cultivation and electricity to several thousand villages whose only light came from candles. The project's showpiece, the huge Dez Dam on the Dezful River, was completed—with a little luck—in 1961.[18] Its reservoirs would provide enough water to irrigate 360,000 acres (145,685 hectares) of new land, literally making the desert bloom.

Projects such as this one helped to give the Iranian people a positive image of the United States and offset—to some degree—the negative image of involvement in the overthrow of Mossadegh. Just as America

The Muhammad Reza Shah Dam provides water and electricity to thousands of villages.

had once sent missionaries to help educate Iranian children, the United States now was sending experts to help Iranians improve their lives.

As an outgrowth of the containment policy toward the Soviet Union, the United States also encouraged Iran to join its neighbors in a regional defense pact.

Thus the Baghdad Pact was formed in 1955, with Iraq, Iran, Pakistan, and Turkey as members. The Iraqi government (also a monarchy) was overthrown by a military coup in 1958, but with American encouragement the pact was renamed the Central Treaty Organization (CENTO), with the same membership, minus Iraq. However, Iranians felt it was another example of foreign power controlling their country's foreign policy. As a result, the United States signed a bilateral agreement with Iran in 1959 that committed American military forces to aid Iran in the event of a Soviet invasion.[19]

Arming the Shah

The U.S. commitment to support the Shah also involved a massive buildup of Iran's armed forces. A strong Iranian military not only would help keep him in power, but it would also provide the glue for the containment of the Soviet Union by a belt of allied countries, Iran being the key country. The policy pleased the Shah, whose ambition was to make Iran the dominant country in the Persian Gulf region.

Over the next decade the United States provided Iran with $500 million in modern weapons, including F-5 and F-4 fighter aircraft, M-60 tanks, missiles, helicopter gunships, and high-powered naval gunboats.[20] More than ten thousand U.S. military personnel were sent to Iran to teach the Iranians how to use this new sophisticated equipment. The other side of the exchange involved bringing thousands of Iranian officers and NCOs to the United States for training at American military bases. There "they learned English, became familiar with modern U.S. military equipment and with U.S. military strategy and tactics, and in the process became somewhat aware of American democratic institutions and principles of government."[21]

The "arming of the Shah" accelerated in the late 1960s and 1970s. One reason was the explosive growth of the Iranian economy. A war between Egypt and Israel in 1973 led the Arab oil-producing countries allied with Egypt to order a shutdown in oil shipments to Europe and the United States, the latter being Israel's ally. As a result, an oil shortage suddenly developed in those areas, and oil prices shot up dramatically. Iranian oil was in much greater demand than it had been, and with the increase in prices, its oil income jumped from $4 billion to $20 billion. The result was the equivalent of the California gold rush, in this case the "black gold" of petroleum, as "prospectors" from American business and industry descended on Iran to relieve the Shah of his new wealth.

The White Revolution

In January 1963 the Shah had introduced, with much fanfare, his personal "White Revolution." It would be "white," that is, carried out without bloodshed or violence, and it would bring about a "revolution" in the lives of his people through new social and economic programs. There were six basic programs: (1) land redistribution; (2) a new election system with voting rights for women; (3) nationalization of all forests; (4) profit sharing for workers in industries; (5) the sale of government-owned monopolies to private investors; and (6) a Literacy Corps. The programs were not original; indeed, several of them had been included in Mossadegh's emergency plan for Iranian social and economic reform. But this time they had the power of the state behind them, plus the backing of the Kennedy administration due to its concern with reform "from the top down" in countries such as Iran.

The Shah introduced his "revolution" for three main reasons. The first was to strengthen his base of popular support as he moved toward becoming absolute ruler of his country. By taking lands away from the "thousand families" who owned more than three fourths of the land used for food production and giving parcels to landless farmers, he would give the latter the motivation and opportunity to improve their lives. And with the addition of reading and writing skills through the Literacy Corps, the Iranian masses would become useful citizens united in support of their ruler.

The second reason for the White Revolution was that it would weaken the power of certain groups, notably the large landowners, to threaten the Shah's power. It would also affect the *ulema* (religious leaders), many of whom were also landowners, managing land and funds donated by rich Muslims in trust for the upkeep of mosques, hospitals, schools, even sacred fountains. In short, the White Revolution would increase state power at the expense of the rest of the society.

The third reason behind the Shah's move to revolutionize Iranian society stemmed from changes in Iran's relationship with the United States. In the 1960 U.S. presidential election, Democrat John F. Kennedy had defeated Richard M. Nixon in a close contest. The Shah, who owed his throne largely to U.S. help and who had developed a good working relationship with the Eisenhower-Nixon team, was counting on a Republican victory. He was understandably concerned

Since Islam has no formal church in the Christian sense of the term, the practice of donating part of one's wealth corresponds to the Christian system of giving to individual churches or denominations. The property so donated is held in irrevocable trust and administered by local religious leaders.

when Kennedy defeated Nixon. The new president in his inaugural address described his foreign policy as one of supporting governments in power as long as they were anti-Communist and would use their power to carry out programs of social and economic development. Such programs, he said, would not only prevent violent revolutions but would also help their people resist communism. The two programs that best illustrated this policy were the Alliance for Progress (designed for Latin America) and the Peace Corps, which would operate throughout the world in non-Communist countries, including Iran.

The first contingent of forty-three Peace Corps volunteers for Iran arrived there in September 1962, and by the end of the program in 1979 some two thousand volunteers had lived and worked there. Most of them were assigned to rural villages, where they lived and worked directly with the people. They spoke Farsi and were well briefed on Iranian customs and values. They also brought practical skills such as building construction, plumbing, teaching English, and irrigation techniques with them. As a result, the Iranian people, especially the rural villagers who made up four fifths of the population, valued the volunteers not only for their skills but also as new friends, interested only in helping them improve their lives.

Peace Corps volunteer Roger Kuhn worked with farmers in Iran, teaching soil preparation, irrigation, pruning, and other agricultural topics.

The Royal Dictator

The White Revolution and the efforts of Peace Corps volunteers brought great changes into Iranian life. But many of these changes came too swiftly, with the result that Iranians were thrown into the modern world without adequate preparation. They needed to adapt the new ways into their traditional Iranian lifestyle without destroying it. The impact of the White Revolution on Iranian society in the long run, however, was less devastating than the impact of modern American culture on the society.

There were some very positive results of the Shah's revolutionary program. Women not only won the right to vote, they also ran for public office, formed women's organizations to push for women's rights similar to those of women in Western countries, and entered the workforce in increasing numbers. Electricity, roads, health clinics, and schools were provided for villages where people lived as they had for centuries, totally out of touch with the outside world. Villagers learned to read and write with the help of volunteers from the Literacy Corps, and thousands of them migrated to the cities in search of work and a new life.

These positive results must be balanced against a number of negative ones. Because the changes had been imposed "from the top down," various groups in society opposed them for different reasons. And the one group that might have become the Shah's main source of support, the educated middle-class professionals—doctors, engineers, journalists, university professors, and experts in various fields—turned against the monarch because of his refusal to develop a multiparty political system with free elections and constitutional limits on his power.

Mohammed Reza Pahlavi was moving in the opposite direction. He saw himself as a modern-day Cyrus the Great, building a great civilization in Iran similar to that of the Persian Empire. His main goal was to gain (and keep) absolute power in the manner of his late father. But whereas Reza Shah had not been obligated to anyone, his son was dependent on the United

States—for the military power that enabled him to rule, and the political support that made it possible for his country to dominate the Persian Gulf region.

Thus the Shah began more and more to play the role of imperial ruler. His third queen, Farah, bore him his first son in 1960, so that there was now a male heir to the Pahlavi dynasty. On October 26, 1967, the Shah's forty-eighth birthday, he held a formal coronation ceremony for himself. In a sharp break with the past, he named Farah regent of the crown. In the event

Although he had ruled for a generation, the Shah delayed his coronation ceremony until 1967 because he did not want to wear the crown until he had accomplished a social revolution in his country.

of his own early death, she would rule Iran on behalf of the seven-year-old crown prince.

In 1971 the Shah outdid himself. He organized a special celebration in the ruins of Persepolis, the ancient Persian capital, to mark the 2,500th anniversary of the monarchy in Iran. The event cost about $200 million. Special tents were set up amid the ancient ruins for foreign heads of state, and meals of roast peacock, crayfish mousse, and other delicacies were prepared by chefs from the famous Maxim's Restaurant in Paris who had been flown in for the occasion. One person attending reported that only the caviar used to stuff quail eggs was Iranian.[22]

The anniversary celebration angered many Iranians not only because of its expense but also because most of them were excluded from attending, as the Shah's troops ringed Persepolis with a security force at checkpoints and roadblocks. Government employees were understandably angered when they were required to contribute a day's pay to meet its expenses. Others felt that the money could have been better spent on the poor and needy or on other projects that would benefit the country. But the Shah's response was that the event had drawn world attention to the world's oldest surviving monarchy.

The event also marked a change in the Shah's policies toward his people. Previously he had combined force with tolerance for opposition groups and moved toward allowing wider participation in the government. In addition to the White Revolution reforms, in 1964 the Shah had set up the *Iran-e-Novin* (New Iran party) as a national political organization, the only one legally allowed in the country. His goal was to attract young, educated professionals (many of them

Iranian soldiers march before dignitaries and heads
of state during a parade marking the 2,500th anniversary
of the Iranian monarchy.

trained at U.S. universities) into the government to
help with his development program. These actions
won him great popularity among officials of three
successive U.S. administrations. He was the favorite
foreign leader of John F. Kennedy, Lyndon B. Johnson,
and Richard M. Nixon. It seemed to them that he was
committed to social reform and eventually a democratic political system. And with U.S. forces increas-
ingly bogged down in Vietnam, a stable, well-armed
Iran would guarantee regional stability in at least one
area of the world.

The "Americanization" of Iran

Any discussion of Iranian-American relations over the 150-odd years of their existence would be incomplete without mention of the effect of American culture, values, and behavior on the people of Iran. As noted earlier in this book, the number of Americans in that country remained relatively small until the 1960s. Most of them were military advisers and Peace Corps volunteers. But the great oil "gold rush," along with the huge weapons purchase program, brought about a large increase in the American population, to more than 50,000, the largest single foreign group in Iran.

Except for the Peace Corps volunteers, who lived on the local economy, most Americans there formed a privileged elite. They lived far better than they had been able to do at home, with salaries up to $120,000 tax free, inexpensive luxury apartments or homes, servants, and cars with drivers. Few of them bothered to learn Farsi. They sent their children to the Tehran American School, and lived mostly in the Iranian counterpart of American suburbs in Tehran and other cities, with fast-food restaurants, pizza parlors, bowling alleys, and theaters showing American movies within easy reach. Tehran and other Iranian cities felt the brunt of this American cultural invasion, with huge neon signs advertising Pepsi and Coca-Cola dominating city skylines and dress shops featuring bikinis and the latest in American fashion along city boulevards. It is not surprising that many Iranians, especially those of the generation that had grown up in the 1940s and 1950s, felt a sense of arrogance on the part of the Americans among them that was primarily cultural.

Ultimately it was the privileged status under the law of the Americans in Iran, rather than their assumed cultural superiority, that would have an extremely bad effect on U.S.-Iranian relations. In 1964 the Majlis passed, under great pressure from the Shah as well as advisers of the U.S. Defense Department, the so-called Status of Forces Act (SOFA). This act exempted American military personnel and their families from liability under Iranian law. Thus an American who ran down and killed an Iranian in a traffic accident (which could easily happen and did in Tehran's appalling traffic congestion) could not be tried in a court of law in Iran for the action. He or she could only be sent home. When the passage of the act was followed immediately by a $200 million loan for new equipment for the Shah's army, most Iranians decided that special treatment for Americans was now a prerequisite for U.S. aid. As the Iranians saw it, America had become the new colonial power, ruling Iran through the Shah for its own selfish interests.[23]

The Shah's Great Enemy

After the fall of Mossadegh, opposition to the Shah was fragmented and lacked leadership. But with the start of the White Revolution the *ulema*, in particular, began organizing in resistance. The land reform affected them because it took donated lands out of their hands to give to landless peasants, while the election reform changed the inferior position of women in Iranian Islamic society by allowing them to vote, work, and hold public office. Many *ulema* members felt that Iran was losing its unique Shia Islamic identity. It was becoming a country ruled by a monarch who was hostile to Islam and was controlled by non-Muslim foreigners.

As had been the case many times in the past, most recently with Mossadegh, a "new Rustam" emerged to save the nation. This Rustam came from the ranks of the *ulema*. He seemed at first glance to be an unlikely hero. Tall, bearded, and unsmiling, a forbidding figure in his black robe and black turban, he was a familiar sight in the halls of the religious seminary at Qum where he taught. His name, taken from the village of his birth, was Rouhollah Moussavi Khomeini. But the Iranian religious community knew him best as Ayatollah Khomeini, *Ayatollah* ("Light of God") being the title given him for his scholarly writings.

Like Mossadegh, Khomeini was in his sixties when he first came to public attention as the leader of the opposition to the Shah. But unlike Mossadegh he had never held public office or involved himself in politics, although he had criticized both Reza Shah and his son in some of his writings and in the classes he taught at the seminary. Consequently, his sudden appearance as an opposition leader came as a surprise to both the Iranian and the American governments.

The White Revolution turned Khomeini into a political activist. Although he was not personally affected since he neither owned nor controlled property, he saw it as a device to destroy the independence of the *ulema*, and in a fiery public speech at the Qum seminary he accused the Shah of trying to weaken Islam. The Shah's response was to have him arrested. He was the first senior member of the *ulema* to be treated in this manner, and there were violent protests throughout the country.

Eventually things calmed down, and Khomeini was released in April 1964. But with the passage of the Status of Forces Act he resumed his attacks on the Shah. In another fiery speech he said, in part: "If someone runs over a dog belonging to an American he will be prosecuted. Even if the Shah himself runs over a dog belonging to an American he will be prosecuted. But if an American cook runs over the Shah, the head of state, no one will have the right to interfere with him."[24]

Khomeini denounced the act as a "document of slavery" for Iran, and went on to attack "the president of the United States" (Lyndon Johnson) as "the most obnoxious person in the world in the eyes of our people, because of the crime he has committed against this nation of Islam," presumably because he forced the Majlis to pass the legislation.

This time the Shah took no chances. Khomeini was again arrested and packed off to Turkey, Iran's neighbor, in exile. But his continued attacks on the head of state of its ally made the Turkish government nervous. In 1965 he was expelled and sent to Iraq. The Iraqi government was in conflict with Iran over border issues and Iranian support for Iraq's rebellious Kurds, and was only too happy to have a sworn enemy of the Shah as its guest. Khomeini was allowed to live in Najaf, an important Shia religious center because it contains the tomb of Ali, Prophet Muhammad's closest relative and revered as the founder of Shia Islam.

During his thirteen-year residence in Najaf, Khomeini continued his attacks on the Shah, gradually gaining widespread popularity among his countrymen for his uncompromising opposition to the tyranny of the ruler. His sermons and speeches were copied on cassette tapes and smuggled into Iran, where they were played or read aloud in village mosques. In 1969 he collected some of them in book form and published them as *Velayet-e-Faqih: Hukumat-e-Islami* (*The Guardianship of the Legal Scholar: Islamic Government*). After the Shah was overthrown and an "Islamic Republic" established in Iran, Khomeini's book provided it with its basic principles of government.

Countdown to Revolution

The growing anti-Shah, anti-American feeling among the Iranian people that would explode in revolution in 1979 was largely unnoticed by U.S. leaders in the 1970's. The close working relationship with the Shah established by presidents Lyndon Johnson, Richard M. Nixon, and Gerald Ford during their administrations, along with the ruler's absolute power and the apparent success of the White Revolution, seemed to outside observers to indicate that the monarch had little to worry about. The Shah in fact took steps to assure Iranian domination of the Gulf region as a means of advancing U.S. policy there. In 1975, with U.S. approval, he signed a peace treaty with Iraq to resolve various issues, notably Iranian support for Iraqi Kurdish rebels. As a result, Khomeini was no longer welcome in Iraq. He was asked to leave that country, and after some hesitation, he was allowed by the French government to settle in France, a country that has a long tradition of giving asylum to political exiles.

Khomeini's move to France seemed to the Shah and U.S. leaders to be an effective means of getting him out of the region. Presumably he would be too far away to have any effect on developments in his country. But as things turned out, the move provided him

Ayatollah Khomeini, during prayers. "Ayatollah" means "Light of God" and was the title given him for his scholarly writings.

and his supporters with a number of advantages. First, as long as he stayed in Iraq, agents of SAVAK, the Shah's secret intelligence service set up and trained by the CIA and Mossad, Israel's foreign spy agency, could "arrange" his mysterious death, as they had done supposedly with his eldest son, Mustafa, during the latter's visit in 1977 to Karbala, another Shia holy city in Iraq. Second, Khomeini was able to contact his supporters and other religious leaders more easily from a Paris base, since he had direct telephone and fax connections with Tehran. And third, his Paris base gave the Ayatollah ready access to the worldwide press, as journalists and reporters virtually camped on his doorstep.

Meanwhile the last U.S. president to deal with Mohammed Reza Shah Pahlavi found himself out of his depth in attempting to formulate an effective policy toward Iran. Jimmy Carter had taken office in 1976 with a strong commitment to human rights. The Shah's dictatorial regime and the ruthless treatment of his political opponents by SAVAK agents did not fit the pattern. But Carter also believed it essential to continue the special U.S. relationship with Iran, since this relationship served U.S. interests in keeping order and assuring oil shipments from the Persian Gulf region. The two foreign-policy objectives obviously contradicted each other.

However, the Shah was able to convince Carter and his advisers that he was indeed willing to improve the human rights situation in Iran and that he was committed to eventually restoring constitutional government. He ordered the release of a large number of political prisoners, invited international human rights organizations such as Amnesty International to "come see for yourselves" how jail conditions and legal procedures had been improved. He also closed down Iran-e-Novin and announced a new political party, Rastakhiz, as a "party for *all* the people."

As the result of these actions, arms sales in Iran by the Carter administration set new records. They also involved highly sophisticated equipment such as AWACS (airborne warning and control system), which carried a price tag of $1.23 billion. Human rights was moved far down the list of issues that might separate the United States from its major ally in the Middle East.

In November 1977 the Shah made his twelfth official visit to the United States. Few thought then that it would be his last as a head of state. He quickly established good personal relations with the president, assuring Carter that the opposition represented a small minority of Iranians. The real need for limits on constitutional government was to keep communism out of the country. A strongly armed Iran was a necessary bulwark against the spread of communism in the region.

Six weeks later Jimmy Carter returned the visit. He stopped in Tehran during a worldwide tour. At a New

U.S. President Jimmy Carter toasts Muhammad Reza Shah.

Year's Eve dinner he toasted the Shah in a short speech:

> Iran, because of the great leadership of Your Majesty, is an island of stability in one of the most troubled areas of the world. This is a great tribute to you, Your Majesty, and to your leadership and the respect and admiration and love which your people give to you. We have no other nation with whom we have closer consultation on regional problems that concern us both. And there is no leader with whom I have a deeper sense of personal gratitude and personal friendship."[25]

Chapter VI

Two Hostile Republics

F ew public statements about the leader of a country by the head of state of its major ally have been as disastrously wrong as President Carter's toast to the Shah. Barely a year later the Iranian monarchy ended abruptly after 2,500 years—its ruler a hunted man seeking asylum in exile and medical treatment for his advanced cancer. Behind him lay a political system in ruins. And with the Shah's departure the United States lost not only its main support base in the Middle East but also its ability to influence, if not control, Iranian foreign policy.

The Islamic Revolution

The 1978–1979 Iranian revolution was one of those events that changed the course of history, not only in Iran but also in Iran's relationships with the United States and other countries. In terms of state formation it may be considered the country's third "revolution" in the twentieth century, the first two being the Constitutional Movement of 1905–1906 and the National Front Movement of 1951–1953. The first two "revolutions" failed to reach their goals. The Constitutional Movement resulted in a document that limited the Shah's power, at least in theory, but when Reza Shah seized power after World War I he ignored it, obeying constitutional rules only when it suited him. The National Front Movement also failed, in that Mossadegh's attempt to restore constitutional government ended in his overthrow and the establishment of absolute power by Muhammad Reza Shah.

The third Iranian revolution has been a success in that it established an Islamic republic to replace the monarchy. It has also discredited the monarchy as a ruling institution in Iran and destroyed the old balance of power between Shahs and the *ulema*. Any return to the days of the Pahlavis, with their open acceptance of Western culture and rejection of traditional Islamic values, is no longer an option, despite increasing evidence, especially among youth, of dissatisfaction with the present religiously ruled regime. The framers and architects of U.S. relations with Iran must therefore develop a policy based on the assumption that the old order has changed indeed, with the *ulema* directly involved in government and social behavior regulated by the laws of Islam.

Opposition to the Shah's dictatorship increased steadily in the 1970s, but opposing groups remained fragmented. This was due largely to the efficient network of spies, agents, and informers of SAVAK that blanketed the country. Even a chance remark criticizing the weather by someone waiting for a bus was sufficient grounds for arrest, if a SAVAK informer happened to be there, and the Shah's prisons filled up with people, ordinary citizens as well as intellectuals and professionals.

The Shah could also count on the loyalty of his army and the support of a small group of business and professional leaders who had made fortunes from Iran's economic growth, and these two groups gave him what seemed to be a solid power base. However, the Ayatollah Khomeini's removal to France in 1978 changed the game. From his base near Paris, Khomeini and his supporters flooded Iran with cassettes, press releases, and faxes denouncing the Shah and calling for his overthrow as a traitor to Islam. The material was smuggled into the country and circulated in cities, towns, and even villages, where preachers in the mosques spread the word in their Friday sermons.

Although the Shah's jails were filled with opponents of his regime, Khomeini's success in reaching more and more of the population with his message made the Shah understandably nervous. With the opposition still disorganized, he decided on a new course of action. It would involve a direct effort to discredit Khomeini. A week after Jimmy Carter's New Year's visit, an article appeared in the progovernment newspaper *Kayhan*. It attacked the Ayatollah by what is usually described as "character assassination," accusing him of not being Iranian (because his grandfather had migrated from India to Iran) and of being a British agent, among other charges. The article had been planted in the newspaper by one of the Shah's press flunkies, and was apparently intended to head off further unrest by discrediting the Ayatollah as a false patriot. But it had the opposite effect, as protest marches and demonstrations spread across the nation.

In the early months of 1978 the marchers were met with force. Still confident of U.S. support for his regime, the Shah ordered his troops and police to crush the protestors. The first "martyrs" of the revolution fell at Qum; like Howard Baskerville in the early years of this century, they died for the cause of freedom in Iran. Among them were mullahs and seminary students. As a result, many members of the *ulema* who had previously stayed out of politics and had not supported Khomeini now joined the anti-Shah forces.

For the rest of the year a cycle of violent action and reaction gripped Iran in an iron vise. In Tabriz, the cradle of the constitutional movement, mobs observing the traditional forty days of mourning in Shia Islam for the martyrs of Qum destroyed liquor stores, billboards with swimsuit advertisements, and other symbols of "decadent" Western culture. On August 19, the anniversary of 28 Mordad, the date of the overthrow of Mossadegh, a fire allegedly set by SAVAK agents in a movie theater in Abadan killed 377 people, most of them women and children. Altogether it is estimated that 10,000 to 12,000 people were killed and 45,000 to 50,000 were injured during fourteen months of revolution.[26]

Despite growing evidence that the Shah was no longer in control of his country, the United States continued to support him. As he wavered between all-out force to crush the opposition and concessions that would reinstate constitutional government, U.S. leaders continued to misread the situation for months. One scholar analyzed the revolution as taking place in four stages: first, protest movements; second, concessions to the opposition balanced with martial law; third, total unification of the opposition and departure of the Shah; and fourth, the collapse of the Pahlavi regime and establishment of an Islamic republic.[27]

As these stages progressed, U.S. policy makers found themselves in disagreement, much as they were during the war in Vietnam. In the case of Iran, the disagreements resulted in failure to develop a coherent policy that would either provide all-out support for the Shah or help him form a coalition government that would save his throne and avoid further violence. Some of Carter's advisers argued that a show of force was needed to bolster the Shah, while others counseled direct contact with Khomeini. But the president continued to believe in the Shah's ability to stay in power for the indefinite future.[28] As late as December 1978, Carter told an interviewer, "I fully expect the Shah to maintain power in Iran and for the present problems in Iran to be resolved."[29]

The Fall of a Monarch

December 11, 1978, marked the anniversary of 'Ashura, the date of the murder of Prophet Muhammad's grandson Husayn, first martyr of Shia Islam, by his enemies in A.D. 680. It has been observed by Shia Muslims ever since as their most important holiday. On that day in 1978 some two million people poured into the streets of Tehran in an all-day protest march. They called for the Shah's overthrow and his replacement by Khomeini. The Shah's army either stood by or dropped their weapons and joined the protestors. Less than a month later the Shah left his country for a final exile. As his father had done, he carried with him a packet of Iranian soil. He had ruled Iran for thirty-seven years and dealt effectively with eight U.S. presidents, and had outlived (or outlasted) most of the world's crowned heads of state. In his years in power, however, he had failed to develop a broad base of support, either through well-meaning programs such as the White Revolution or for his leadership. Iran's vast oil revenues had brought great wealth to a few, but little prosperity to the majority of his people. Now the *mostazafin*, "the oppressed," slum dwellers, the down-trodden masses, exploded out of their slums in a massive show of support for the Ayatollah Khomeini. And in his hour of greatest need, the Shah's U.S. backers failed him.

The Islamic Republic

With the Shah's departure Khomeini returned and announced the end of the monarchy, which he said was incompatible with Islam. Henceforth, Iran would be an Islamic republic, a *theocracy*, that is, a political

The Ayatollah leaves France to fly to Iran

and form an Islamic republic.

system in which government is controlled by religious leaders. Khomeini had laid out the principles of this system in his book on Islamic government. The key term in the system is the *velayet-e-faqih* ("guardianship of the wise jurist"), which provides for authority over the people to be held by a religious leader who is superior to all others in wisdom and understanding of God's will. Just as Prophet Muhammad was the representative of God for the Muslims of his time, the *faqih* is God's representative to the Shia Muslim community and is therefore responsible only to God.

The basic difference between the Islamic republic of Iran and the American republic stems from this concept. In the U.S. system, laws are made by elected representatives of the American people to reflect the majority will. In Iran, laws are believed to come ultimately from God. They must conform to God's will as expressed in the Koran and as interpreted by the *faqih* in order to be valid.

Except for its dependence upon Islamic law and the role and position of the *faqih*, the Islamic republic is like other republics in having a constitution that divides government into three branches: executive, legislative, and judicial. It has a president with a cabinet of ministers who head various government departments, similar in structure to the U.S. government. The legislative branch consists of the Majlis, which has been a fixture in Iranian politics since its founding in 1906. Majlis deputies are elected by universal adult suffrage. The minimum voting age is fifteen, a reflection of Iran's extremely youthful population. The judiciary is in theory independent, with the right to appeal, and the judicial review process is written into the constitution. There is no bill of rights as such, but the constitution protects the right to private property, and guarantees economic rights, such as social security, health insurance, free education, and other welfare benefits. It also commits the government to establish a balanced budget.

However, all laws and guaranteed rights are subject to Islamic law as interpreted by the *faqih*. In practice this has meant the application of strict moral standards to the people. These standards are under the control of two special groups, the Revolutionary Guards (a special police force set up by Khomeini to defend the revolution against its perceived internal enemies) and the Komitehs, similar to morality squads or neighborhood watch committees. Although Khomeini was not opposed to constitutional government, he insisted that Islamic government, unlike Western constitutional governments, has a moral and social responsibility for the behavior of Muslims. "Islam," he said, "has commandments for everybody, everywhere, in any place, in any condition. If a person were to commit an immoral dirty deed right next to his house, Islamic governments have business with him."[30]

The Komitehs and Revolutionary Guards have enforced these standards with varying degrees of strictness. During the Khomeini decade they were directed primarily against women. The dismantling of women's rights, as they had developed under the Shah, began with annulment of the Family Protection Law of 1967, which had enabled women to work outside the home and set the age of consent for marriage at eighteen, among other protective benefits.[31] Now veils became obligatory for women working in government offices, and the veil, head scarf, and chador (a long shapeless robe) became the mandatory costume for women in public. These restrictions have continued; special "vice squads" patrol city streets on the lookout for "moral offenses" against Islam, such as boys and girls walking hand in hand, and raiding bazaars and shopping malls to arrest anyone not wearing correct Islamic dress—"nail polish and Reebok shoes are treated as lethal weapons," one reporter noted.[32]

In view of the hostility of the Islamic republic toward America, a brief analysis of the Iranian constitution underlines the basic differences between the political systems of the two republics. The preamble to the Iranian constitution states that the republic is based on the justice of God, the existence of God and submission (Islam) to His will; the fundamental role of God's will in human laws; and the vesting of authority over His people in the *ulema*. The constitution was drawn up by an assembly of experts (all religious leaders) in 1980, revised several times, and issued in final form in 1989 after Khomeini's death. The model for the revised version is not the U.S. Constitution but that of the French Republic, with a strong executive, a national parliament responsible for budget and laws, and an independent judiciary. As is the case in France, the accused in a court case is guilty until proven innocent, and during the Khomeini years special courts outside the judiciary system were set up to try members of the Shah's regime for anti-Islamic activities. They did their job with such thoroughness that the presiding justice was given the name "Hanging Judge" for his role in the process. But since these excesses were ended, largely on Khomeini's orders, the Iranian legal system has functioned much like that of the United States except for continued restrictions on women's rights and the role of the *velayet-e-faqih* as final authority over the law.[33]

The Great Satan

In the beginning of this book it was noted that the "hostage crisis" of 1979–1981 was the first event in the recent history of U.S.–Iranian relations to bring nationwide awareness of Iran and its people to Americans. The yellow ribbons that sprouted on Americans' front doors showed not only the support for the hostages in their ordeal but also the depth of American anger toward Iran. But the U.S. public and government failed to judge the depth and intensity of the

Even Iranian students in the United States had intense anti-Shah feelings. In Washington, D.C., students burned a picture of the Shah in front of the White House while the Shah was there on an official visit.

Iranians' anti-Shah feelings and anger toward the United States for its continued backing of the Iranian monarch. When the Shah was admitted to the United States for medical treatment of what proved to be his terminal illness, this Iranian anger toward the United States reached a climax. The Khomeini government had advised restraint, but there were ample warnings from students, the group most strongly committed to the revolution, that some sort of strong anti-American event was to come.

The Shah entered the United States on October 22, 1979, and militant students seized the U.S. Embassy on November 4. They ignored the rules of international law, which specify that embassies in a country are exempt from occupation by the host country, and held the Embassy and its fifty-three resident staff members as hostages for the next 444 days. The students brushed aside the U.S. claim that the Shah had been admitted for humanitarian reasons as a kindness to him in his last days. They said the Embassy was a "nest of spies," and that the United States had admitted the Shah to help restore him to power as they had done in Operation Ajax. To make their point, the students brought out some sixty volumes of Embassy reports that they said would "prove" that America was ruling Iran rather than the Shah.[34]

Khomeini seems to have been taken by surprise by the occupation; he had not authorized it, although the students said they were acting in his name. But ever the opportunist, Khomeini threw his weight behind it, realizing it would give Iran some leverage against the expected American countercoup. As a result, Iranian-American relations entered a new ice age. The United States now became the "Great Satan," the personifica-

**An American hostage is paraded before cameras
by his Iranian captors in 1979.**

tion of evil working through a superpower to destroy
the revolution.

Since the expected countercoup did not take place,
and the one attempt to rescue the hostages by an airborne mission ended in disaster in a desert sandstorm,
Iranians viewed the occupation of the Embassy as a
victory. Khomeini said that God had thrown sand into
the motors of the American helicopters to protect a
nation ruled by Islam! When the hostages were finally
released, on Inauguration Day 1981, a new U.S. president had taken office and Iran had become for Americans their most hated nation. Ironically, sanctuary for
the Shah was now irrelevant. Muhammad Reza

Pahlavi had become a refugee, wandering from country to country. He died in Egypt, the only country that would accept him, on July 27, 1980, and was buried next to his father in a Cairo cemetery.

The release of the hostages and the defeat of Jimmy Carter, the American president most closely associated with the Shah, might have been expected to bring a thaw in the icy U.S.–Iranian relationship. But Ronald Reagan came to the White House riding tall in the saddle like the cowboy actor he once was, determined to punish "outlaw nations" like Iran and restore American prestige abroad. An inexpensive and easy way to do so would be to provide arms and military equipment to their neighbors, in effect using these neighboring countries as proxies to bring these outlaws to heel. In Iran's case, its neighbor Iraq had invaded it in 1980 and occupied a large chunk of its territory. The United States began supplying Iraq with modern weapons to update its mostly obsolete Soviet equipment. As a result, Iraq's army was much better equipped than Iran's and won a series of victories in the early stages of the war. The Iranians managed to stave off total defeat, but they desperately needed modern weapons to match the Iraqis.

The Reagan administration's "tilt" toward Iraq ended abruptly in 1987, when Iraqi planes bombed and sank the U.S. naval frigate *Stark* in the Persian Gulf, killing thirty-seven American sailors. Iraq's president, Saddam Hussein, called the attack a tragic mistake and promised compensation to the families of those killed. However, the likelihood of further "accidents" to American warships in that hotly contested waterway led Reagan's military advisers to argue that aid to Iraq should be balanced with increased military assistance to Iran. Their assumption was that there were moderates in the Iranian government who would be encouraged to seek a better relationship with the United States, thus helping to protect American strategic interests in the Gulf. This policy brought about the ill-fated "Iran-Contra" operation, a secret approach through contacts with these so-called moderates. The United States would send arms to Iran in return for their help in obtaining the release of American hostages held in Lebanon by a Shia group supposedly armed and financed by the Iranian government. The funds for payment of the arms would then be transferred from Iran to the government of Nicaragua (the "Contras"), a U.S. ally in Central America, to help it overcome a Communist-led rebellion there. But in the same way as the hostage rescue mission had failed because of human miscalculations, the Iran-Contra "arms for hostages" plan fell apart when anti-American officials in the Iranian government exposed it to the world press. As one scholar observed, it involved "the wrong people in the wrong place at the wrong time, resulting in a deep freeze in U.S.-Iranian relations for at least another decade."[35]

Surviving Khomeini

In February 1999 the Islamic Republic of Iran marked its twentieth anniversary. It had already overcome a number of problems that might easily have destroyed a weaker or less well-entrenched regime. Its first two decades of existence were scarred by war and violent internal conflicts, and its isolation as an "outlaw nation" due to U.S. policy caused economic and social hardships.

The republic's initial problem was a war with Iraq, which broke out barely a year after the revolution. Iraq's leaders assumed that the Shah's overthrow and the apparent collapse of his army would give them an easy victory. Success would make Iraq the dominant power in the Persian Gulf region. Initially, Iraqi forces won a number of victories and occupied most of the westernmost Iranian province of Khuzistan. However, the mainly Arab population of that province failed to rise in support of the invasion, preferring a distant Iranian regime to the ruthless dictatorship of Saddam Hussein. With its own land in danger, the battered Iranian army regrouped and gradually drove back the invaders. Encouraged by Khomeini's unrelenting hatred for Iraq's leaders as "Godless enemies of Islam," thousands of young Iranian volunteers, many of them twelve or thirteen years old, rushed to fight the enemy. A UN-sponsored cease-fire in 1988 finally halted the conflict. Losses on both sides were heavy; in Iran's case with over 400,000 killed and a million men wounded. Khuzistan, where in the Shah's time American experts had developed a prosperous economy based on wheat production and oil, had become a desolate place where nothing grew. The ground was thickly sown with land mines, and villages were abandoned by their inhabitants.

In Iran itself there were different views of the purpose and objectives of the revolution, as Communists, nationalists, and members of other groups that had united to carry it out fought to impose their goals and ideologies on the nation. Khomeini held the country together almost alone, changing his position and views from time to time in order to keep any one group from becoming too powerful at the expense of

Iranian children sit in front of a picture of the Ayatollah Khomeini during prayers held at Tehran University after his death.

the others. As the Supreme Guide, he stayed above political conflict as the final source of truth and authority. When he died in 1989 at the age of eighty-six, the entire nation mourned. A member of the Majlis said of him: "Much like the Holy Prophet Abraham, he carried out God's Will, smashed idols, was willing to sacrifice his own son, rose up against tyrants, and led the oppressed against their oppressors."[36]

What Price Reconciliation?

In theory, Khomeini's death should have given both the United States and Iran an opportunity to rethink their views of each other. The tall, brooding figure in the black turban had been a major obstacle to reconciliation, given his rigid hostility to America as the Shah's main backer and his conviction that every plot to overthrow the republic had American hands behind it. But since his death there has been no thaw in the freeze in official relations. The closest thing to government-to-government contacts thus far is the U.S.–Iran Claims Tribunal. It was set up after the revolution to handle claims by American companies against Iran and Iranian claims for U.S. military and other equipment ordered by the Shah's government but never delivered. The tribunal, located in The Hague (Netherlands), has not been affected by political differences between the two countries and has been able to settle a large number of claims. By 1996, $6 billion had been awarded to U.S. companies and $4 billion to Iran for undelivered equipment.

Otherwise, official relations are handled by intermediaries. Iran is represented in the United States by the Embassy of Algeria in Washington, and the United States by the Swiss Embassy in Tehran. The U.S. government policy of arming Iraq during the 1980–1988 war further alienated Iranian leaders; the "Great

Satan" seemed responsible for early Iraqi successes and for the slaughter of lightly armed Iranian teenagers by superior Iraqi weaponry.

During the Khomeini years and the two terms of his protégé Ali Akbar Hashemi Rafsanjani as president (1989–1997), the Iranian government worked actively to promote its version of "Islamic revolution" abroad, supporting efforts by groups in other Islamic countries to overthrow those regimes considered non-Islamic—that is, not true to the sacred law of Islam in their conduct and policies. This policy led U.S. policy makers to brand Iran as a "nest of terrorists." The action that galled Americans more than any other was the kidnapping of U.S. citizens in Beirut, the capital of Lebanon, by Shia Muslim groups supposedly financed and directed by the Islamic Republic.

Changes in internal Iranian politics and the country's increasing openness in foreign policy have not generated any U.S. changes or response. Iran stayed neutral during the 1991 Gulf War, even interning Iraqi pilots and their planes after they had flown there to escape Allied attacks. Undeterred, President Bill Clinton in 1995 ordered a trade embargo, similar to sanctions, on the republic. Subsequently, Congress passed a bill that would penalize not only American but also foreign companies that invested $40 million or more in Iranian development projects. The bill aroused a storm of opposition abroad. European oil companies planning to enter the Iranian market said they would not be bound by its terms, and the UN-affiliated World Trade Organization warned that it would file suit against the U.S. government for violation of free-trade rights in the global market. Pressure from the European Union made enforcement of the bill unlikely, and in 1999 the Clinton administration waived sanctions against three foreign oil companies (Total of France, Gazprom of Russia, and Petronas of Malaysia), which are developing the huge South Pars gas field in the Persian Gulf. But the embargo effectively discouraged American companies from returning to Iran in a nonpolitical capacity to help it recover economically from the war with Iraq. As one example, the U.S. oil company Conoco had signed a major contract to develop newly discovered southern Iranian oil fields but canceled the contract in order to avoid fines of up to $40 million for violations of the embargo. The development contract then went to Total of France.

Continued U.S. hostility toward Iran has failed to take into account important changes in Iran's political configuration in the 1990s. In 1997, Mohammed Khatami, a lower-ranking member of the *ulema* and a former minister of culture, was elected to succeed Rafsanjani as president. He won a landslide and unexpected victory; he defeated the Speaker of the Majlis (Parliament), who had been the preferred choice of the religious leaders and had been expected to win handily. Khatami's 69 percent majority resulted in a large measure from massive support by women and young voters, groups that deeply resented Islamic restrictions on their personal behavior and the country's failure to improve the economy. Since that election a fierce debate has raged between those who favor a more open, liberal society with access to the outside world, and those who insist on continued direct rule by the *ulema*. To put it another way, the debate is between those who would encourage free expression and fewer restrictions on behavior, dress, and other social aspects of Iranian Islam, and those who insist on

Mohammed Khatami listens to reporters during his first news conference as Iran's president-elect. Khatami received 20 million votes out of 29 million votes cast.

rigid obedience to Islamic law and custom in all phases of life: social moderates or modernists versus hard-line Islamic conservatives. As one young Iranian told a reporter, "Everywhere you go someone is telling you what to do, your family, your school, the police, the Komiteh, all of them forcing Islam down your throat."[37]

Obviously the United States cannot and should not become involved or take sides in this debate. Nor would it be appropriate for us to demand that the proud Iranian nation behave as we think it should, in accordance with our democratic principles and cherished human rights. The job of improving Iranian-American relations—thawing the deep freeze between the United States and its former friend and ally—is made especially difficult by the high level of paranoia in Iranian politics and the Iranian view of the outside world, commented on by outside observers as far back as the 1800s.[38] Yet this paranoia has not kept the Iranian people from nonpolitical overtures toward their onetime "Great Friend."

Most of these overtures have been made since Khatami's election. In 1998 the American winner of the 118-pound World Wrestling Championships, held in Tehran, was saluted with the "Star-spangled Banner," played by an Iranian band, while the Stars and Stripes waved proudly alongside the Iranian flag. U.S. travel agencies have sponsored a number of tours to Iran—with mixed results.[39] And although official relations remain frozen, the U.S. State Department in 1999 removed Iran from its list of countries that actively sponsor terrorism worldwide.

In an address to the Asia Society in New York City, U.S. Secretary of State Madeleine Albright noted that what is needed is a new "road map" to restore friendship and ties between our two nations. Actions that build confidence on both sides would help lay out roads for this map. As examples, the Clinton administration could approve a request by an American company to sell grain and sugar to Iran to meet an Iranian shortfall in its production of these crops. The administration could also ease current restrictions on imports of Iranian carpets. Such actions (which do not require congressional approval) would go a long way toward building confidence among Iranians that the United States wishes only to revive the ancient friendship, with no ulterior motives. The food sale would make it easier for the Iranian government to subsidize these basic foods for Iranian families suffering from loss of income as a result of low world oil prices. Increased carpet exports from Iran to the United States, its largest customer, would enable the Iranian carpet industry to expand, creating many new jobs. And with the new road map in place, not only Iranian-American friendship, but prospects for real peace in an unstable area of the world would be greatly improved.

Source Notes

1. Yonah Alexander, and Allan Nanes, eds., *Iran: A Documentary History.* Frederick, MD: University Publications of America, 1980, p. 2.

2. John Boyle, ed., *Persia: History and Culture.* London: Henry Melland, 1978, pp. 29–30.

3. John W. Limbert, *Iran: At War With History.* Boulder, CO: Westview Press, 1987, p. 49.

4. Limbert, p. 80.

5. Arthur C. Millspaugh, *Americans in Persia.* Washington, D.C.: Brookings Institution, 1946, p. 23.

6. Donald N. Wilber, *Reza Shah.* Hicksville, NY: Exposition Press, 1975, p. 204.

7. Joel Sayre, *Persian Gulf Command.* New York: Random House, 1943, a personal memoir by a *New Yorker* reporter.

8. Millspaugh, p. 263.

9. Ibid.

10. The would-be assassin fired six shots from close range at the Shah as he was entering the University of Tehran to attend a graduation ceremony. The Shah was wounded in the cheek and shoulder but was otherwise

unhurt, as he danced and shadowboxed in front of his attacker. *Tehran Journal*, October 26, 1967.

11. He said he had burned it because it had been imposed on Iran at "the time of ignorance." *Memoirs of Mohammad Musaddiq*, ed. by Homa Katouzian. London: JEBHE, 1988, p. 287.

12. See Farah Diba, *Mohammad Mossadegh*. London: Croom Helm, 1986, p. 102. The company even sent a leaflet to the Shah and the prime minister titled, "A Child's Guide to the Agreement," implying that they could only understand something written for children.

13. Ambassador John C. Wiley, quoted in George McGhee, *Envoy to the Middle World: Adventures in Diplomacy*. New York: Harper & Row, 1983, p. 73.

14. Dean Acheson, *Present at the Creation*. New York: W. W. Norton, 1969, pp. 650–651.

15. Donald N. Wilber, *Adventures in the Middle East: Excursions and Incursions*, Princeton, NJ: Darwin Press, 1986, p. 188, quoting Kermit Roosevelt.

16. Wilber, *Adventures in the Middle East*, p. 189.

17. He died in 1967 at the age of eighty-five, insisting to the end of his life that his sole aim was that "the people of Iran enjoy independence and dignity and are not subjected to anybody's rule except the will of the majority." *Memoirs of Mohammad Musaddiq*, p. 259.

18. In his Musaddiq autobiography, *Mission for My Country*, New York: McGraw-Hill, 1961, the Shah wrote: "Pouring concrete started in 1958 when for luck I threw coins into the first bucket," p. 147.

19. For the text of the agreement, see Alexander and Nanes, pp. 306–307.

20. Robert Pranger and Dale Tahtinen, *United States Policy in the Persian Gulf*. Washington, D.C.: American Enterprise Institute, 1979, p. 7.

21. "Landlords had previously been able to rely on their peasants both as troops for their private armies and as voters able to help guarantee their election to the Majlis." Marvin Zonis, *Majestic Failure: The Fall of the Shah.* Chicago: University of Chicago Press, 1991, p. 108.

22. See Cynthia Helms, *An Ambassador's Wife in Iran*, New York: Dodd, Mead, & Company, 1980, p. 69, for a detailed description of the celebration.

23. James Bill, *The Eagle and the Lion: The Tragedy of American-Iranian Relations.* New Haven: Yale University Press, 1988, p. 158. In a 1966 interview an Iranian told a visitor: "Isn't this why you fought the British? The redcoats refused to abide by local law in the colonies. Why do Americans insist on being above the law in Iran?"

24. Quoted in Bill, pp. 159–160.

25. Princess Ashraf Pahlavi, *Faces in a Mirror: Memoirs from Exile.* Englewood Cliffs, NJ: Prentice-Hall, 1980, p. 1.

26. These totals were calculated by the Foundation of Martyrs, which was set up to distribute funds to families who lost one or more members during the uprising.

27. Sepehr Zabih, *Iran's Revolutionary Upheaval: An Interpretive Essay.* San Francisco: Alchemy Books, 1979, pp. 45–71.

28. CIA and Defense Intelligence reports as late as September 1978 projected that the Shah would continue in power well into the 1980s.

29. Quoted in Bill, p. 259. Carter's 1978 statements about Iran were later published in the February 1979 issue of *Afro-Asian Affairs* magazine.

30. Hamid Dabashi, *Theology of Discontent.* New York: New York University Press, 1993, pp. 476–477.

31. Khomeini had argued before the revolution that voting rights for women were un-Islamic. After the revolution

he said that to deprive women of these rights was un-Islamic!

32. Azar Nafisi, "The Veiled Threat," *New Republic*, February 22, 1999, p. 28.

33. John Simpson, and Tina Shubart, *Lifting the Veil: Life in Revolutionary Iran*. London: Hodder & Stoughton, 1995, p. 140.

34. The minister of environmental affairs in Khatami's present cabinet, and his first woman appointee, was the chief spokesperson for the student militants during the hostage crisis. Donna Hughes, "Women in Iran," Z magazine, October 1998, p. 23.

35. Bill, p. 313.

36. Kayhan newspaper, June 21, 1989, quoted in Ervand Abrahamian, *Khomeinism: Essays on the Islamic Republic*. Berkeley: University of California Press, 1993, p. 13.

37. Colin Barraclough, in *The Christian Science Monitor*, April 2, 1997.

38. Cf. Lord Curzon, *Persia and the Persian Question*. London: Longman's 1892.: "They are a suspicious people. They see a cloven hoof beneath the skirt of every robe," p. 631.

39. In 1998 a busload of American businessmen was attacked while on their way from the airport to their hotel by young men. Wielding clubs and bats, they smashed the bus windows, shouting, "God is great! Death to America!" According to a hard-line Iranian newspaper, the reason for the attack was that the American group included spies disguised as tourists. The newspaper article added: "Your children performed the first operation against American spies. There were no injuries, but it was a chilling reminder that Iran is not a benign place to visit." Elaine Sciolino, in *The New York Times*, February 28, 1999.

Iran Facts

Geography

Area: 636,294 square miles (1,648,000 square kilometers), about the size of Alaska and Pennsylvania combined

Capital: Tehran (population 6,500,000)

Borders on: Afghanistan, Armenia, Azerbaijan, Iraq, Pakistan, Turkey

Climate: arid or semiarid, subtropical along Caspian Sea coast

Topography: rugged mountains along northwestern region, high central basin with huge deserts and discontinuous mountain ranges

Elevation: lowest: Caspian Sea, 92 feet (28 meters), highest: Mt. Demavend, 18,607 feet (5,671 meters)

Natural Resources: petroleum, natural gas, coal, chromium, copper, sulfur

People

Population: 68,959,931 (1998)

Growth Rate: 1.8 percent

Birthrate: 31.37 per 1,000

Death Rate: 6.19 per 1,000

Infant Mortality: 55 per 1,000 live births

Life Expectancy: 68 (at birth); males 66.8, females 69.7

Ethnic Groups: Persian 51 percent, Azerbaijani Turkish 24 percent, Gilaki/Mazanderani 8 percent, Kurds 7 percent, others 10 percent

Religions: Shia Muslim 89 percent, Sunni Muslim 10 percent, others 1 percent

Languages: Farsi spoken by majority of people; others are Azeri Turkish, Kurdish

Adult Literacy Rate: 72 percent overall, males 78 percent, females 65.8 percent

Government

Type: theocratic republic

Independence Date: April 1, 1979

Flag: 3 equal horizontal bands of green (top), white (middle), and red (bottom); the national emblem, a stylized version of the word Allah, written in red in center of white band; the phrase Allah Akbar ("God Is

Great") is repeated in white Arabic script along bottom of green band and across top edge of red band

Head of State: Supreme Guide Ayatollah Ali Hoseini-Khamenei; President Mohammed Khatami (also prime minister)

Political Parties: presently banned. Political associations, which may submit candidates for the Majlis for approval by the Council of Constitutional Guardians, include Tehran Militant Clergy, Militant Clerics Association, Servants of Reconstruction (headed by ex-President Rafsanjani).

The republic also allows pressure groups to form that are either for or opposed to the election process. Pro-government groups include Ansar-e-Hezbollah, Mojahedin of the Islamic Revolution, Muslim Students Following the Imam's Line, Islamic Coalition Association. The Liberation Movement of Iran and the Nation of Iran are opposition groups legally allowed to function.

Legislature: Majlis e-Shura-ye-Islami (Islamic Consultative Assembly), unicameral, 270 seats, members elected for 4-year terms, in existence since 1906

Most recent election: 1996

Suffrage: universal at age 15

Military

Number of Armed Forces: 640,000

Military Expenditures (percent of Central Government Expenditures): 13.6 percent

Age for Mandatory Military Service: 21

Economy

Currency: rial. Official rate 3,000 rials equals U.S. $1; black market (free) rate 4,600 rials equals $1

Per Capita Income: $4,720, on basis of $310 billion in Gross Domestic Product (GDP)

Total Foreign Debt: $30 billion

Agricultural Resources: rice, barley, wheat, sugar beets, cotton, dates, pistachios

Industries: petroleum refining, petrochemicals, textiles, cement, food processing, production of tanks, small arms, and other weapons

Labor Force: 15,250,000; shortage of skilled labor due to Iraq war

Unemployment: 30 percent

Foreign Trade

Exports: $19 billion (1997)

Imports: $15.6 billion (1997)

Bibliography

Abrahamian, Ervand. *The Iranian Mojahedin*. New Haven: Yale University Press, 1989.

———. *Khomeinism: Essay on the Islamic Republic*. Berkeley: University of California Press, 1993.

Afary, Janet. *The Iranian Constitutional Revolution 1906–1911: Grassroots Democracy, Social Democracy, & the Origins of Feminism (History and Society of the Mode)*. New York: Columbia University Press, 1996.

Bill, James A. *The Eagle and the Lion: The Tragedy of Iranian-American Relations*. New Haven: Yale University Press, 1988.

Bill, James A., and Louis W. Roger, eds. *Musaddiq, Iranian Nationalism and Oil*. Austin: University of Texas Press, 1988.

Cook, J. M. *The Persian Empire*. London: J. M. Dent, 1983.

Cordesman, Anthony. *The Iran-Iraq War and Western Security 1984–87*. London: Janes's Publishing Company, 1987.

Ehteshami, Anoushirvan. *After Khomeini: The Iranian Second Republic*. London: Routledge & Kegan Paul, 1995.

Forbis, William. *Fall of the Peacock Throne: The Story of Iran.* New York: Harper & Row, 1980.

Fuller, Graham. *Center of the Universe, the Geopolitics of Iran.* Boulder, CO: Westview Press, 1991.

Garthwaite, Gene. *Khans and Shahs: The Bakhtiyari in Iran.* Cambridge, England: Cambridge University Press, 1983.

Ghani, Cyrus. *Iran and the Rise of Reza Shah.* London: I. B. Tauris, 1998.

Goode, James F. *The U.S. and Iran: In the Shadow of Musaddiq.* New York: St. Martin's Press, 1997.

Hiro, Dilip. *Iran Under the Ayatollahs.* London: Routledge & Kegan Paul, 1985.

Kamrava, Mehran. *The Political History of Iran: From Tribalism to Theocracy.* New York: Praeger, 1992.

Katouzian, Homa. *Musaddiq and the Struggle for Power in Iran.* London: I. B. Tauris, 1990.

Limbert, John W. *Iran: At War With History.* Boulder, CO: Westview Press, 1987.

Mohammed Reza Pahlavi, Shah of Iran. *Answer to History.* New York: Stein & Day, 1980.

———. *Mission for My Country.* New York: McGraw-Hill. 1961.

Pelletierre, Stephen. *The Iran-Iraq War: Chaos in a Vacuum.* New York: Praeger, 1992.

Ramazani, R. K., ed. *Iran's Revolution: The Search for Consensus.* Bloomington: Indiana University Press, 1990.

Savory, Roger. *Iran Under the Safavids.* Cambridge, England: Cambridge University Press, 1980.

Spencer, William. *Iran: Land of the Peacock Throne.* New York: Benchmark Books, 1997.

Wilbur, Donald N. *Reza Shah*. Hicksville, NY: Exposition Press, 1975.

Wright, Robin. *In the Name of God: The Khomeini Decade*. New York: Simon and Schuster, 1989.

Zonis, Marvin. *Majestic Failure: The Fall of the Shah*. Chicago: University of Chicago Press, 1991.

Page numbers in *italics* refer to illustrations.